The Peoples' Voice

DOMINICAN REPUBLIC

Culture and History

The Peoples Publishing Group, Inc.

Free to Learn, to Grow, to Change

Created in the Rochester City School District
Rochester, New York

The Peoples Publishing Group, Inc.

Free to Learn, to Grow, to Change

ISBN 1-56256-030-1

Table of Contents

The Seal of The Dominican Republic

The Island of the Dominican Republic

To the Teacher

This book, one in a series of three books, provides students with information about the history and culture of the Dominican Republic. The other books in the series focus on Cuba and Puerto Rico. The series was written because the history, culture and contributions of Latin American people are often omitted or misrepresented in textbooks and other instructional materials. These three countries were chosen because they are the lands of origin of a significant number of people who live in the United States, including a large number of students who attend our school system.

The series is the result of recommendations made in the Hispanic Studies Task Force A.H.O.R.A. Report (Access for Hispanics to Opportunities Results in Achievement) (1986). The A.H.O.R.A. Report emphasized the importance of curriculum materials which include the history and contributions of Latino people, and thus enable students to grow in knowledge and appreciation of themselves and others. In response to this recommendation, the development of supplemental materials on Latin America became an initiative of the Curriculum Development and Support Department. After careful analysis of current District elementary textbooks, it was clear that the issues, events and contributions of Latin American people were not treated with sufficient objectivity and depth. Since the United States has historically had important relationships with the Dominican Republic, Cuba and Puerto Rico, students can benefit from a deeper understanding of these countries.

Although the three countries highlighted in this series have much in common, each has distinctive characteristics. Thus, you will find the treatment of similar topics in each book, as well as the treatment of topics specific to each country. The series is not intended to be a definitive history of three countries. Its role is to provide youngsters with information that is not usually available, and to do this in a way which respects the cultures being presented. Each book has selected historical events and issues that have determined to be most significant.

This book is written in chronological order, beginning with the history and culture of the country's original inhabitants. All chapters have review sections including vocabulary, lesson review questions, critical thinking and writing and enrichment exercises. Several vignettes are included to provide focused treatment of particular topics. The index and glossary in each book should also be helpful to your students.

Great care has been taken to avoid the biased terminology we inherit from earlier time periods. An example would be the term "Indian," which resulted from an error on the part of Columbus and does not accurately identify any group of original inhabitants in the Americas. Footnotes or content explanations are included when terms that may not be familiar to students are used.

Essential to the development of this series is the use of an indigenous cultural orientation. In other words, an attempt was made to write the history and culture of each country from the "eyes" of the culture, rather than from outside perspectives. To achieve this internal orientation, a writer from each country served as the primary writer. In addition, in conducting their research, the writers drew upon many scholarly works by historians from within and outside of each country. A bibliography of these works is included at the end of each book.

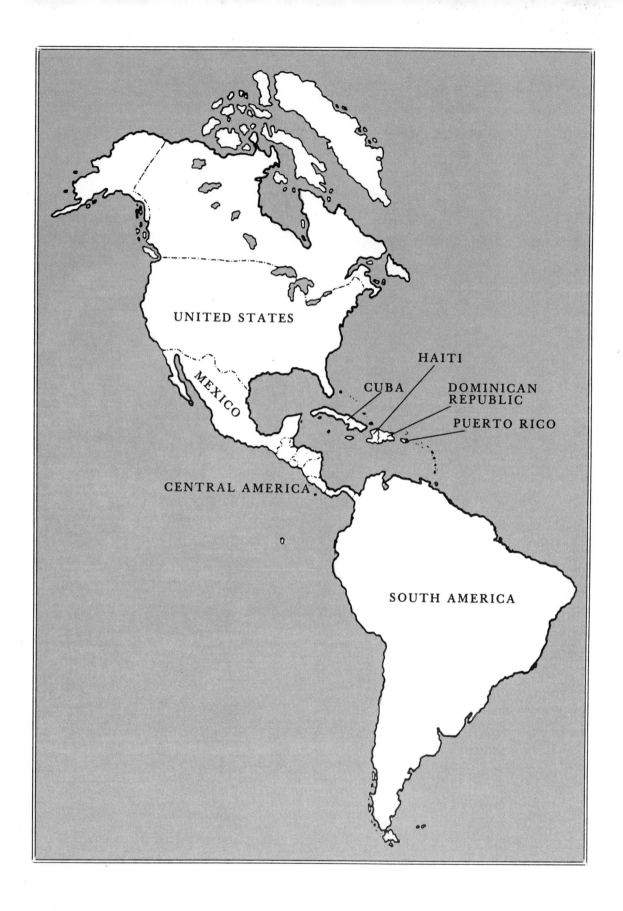

To the Student

This book is one book in a series about the history and culture of three countries: Cuba, the Dominican Republic and Puerto Rico. As you look at the map of the Americas on the opposite page, you can see how close the United States is to Cuba, the Dominican Republic and Puerto Rico. This is one reason why the United States has long-standing relationships with each of these countries. It is important for all of us to have accurate and up-to-date information about our neighbors. This book will help to provide that information.

This book is about the Dominican Republic. The first chapter describes the country's early history. You will learn a lot about the original inhabitants and their way of life. You will also learn about the arrival and impact of African and European people. Today, the people of the Dominican Republic are mostly a blend of the original inhabitants, Africans and Europeans.

There may not be enough time to read and discuss this whole book in class. Thus, you may wish to use this book for outside reading or as a resource for special projects.

INTRODUCTION TO
THE DOMINICAN REPUBLIC

  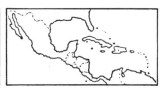 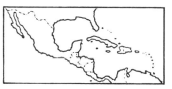

The heritage of the Dominican people dates back several thousand years. The original inhabitants of the island, the Ciboney and Taíno peoples, called their island Haití or Quisqueya. In 1492, Spain "claimed" the island and changed its name to Hispaniola. Spaniards exploited both the original people and African people who lived there, in their attempts to develop a prosperous colony. Over time, the blend of Ciboney, Taíno, Spanish, and diverse African cultures influenced aspects of daily life such as language, religion, art, architecture, food, dance, and music.

After a long struggle, Dominicans were able to achieve independence in 1844. They worked hard to develop their country, and to resist and throw off domination by other countries. There was a steady effort to gain more freedom and human rights. Today Dominicans enjoy many of these rights. As leaders and citizens approach the twenty first century, they are linked together in the struggle to shape a strong social, political, and economic future for the Dominican Republic.

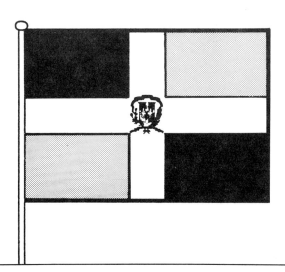

CHAPTER

1

The Original Inhabitants of the República Dominicana (The Dominican Republic)

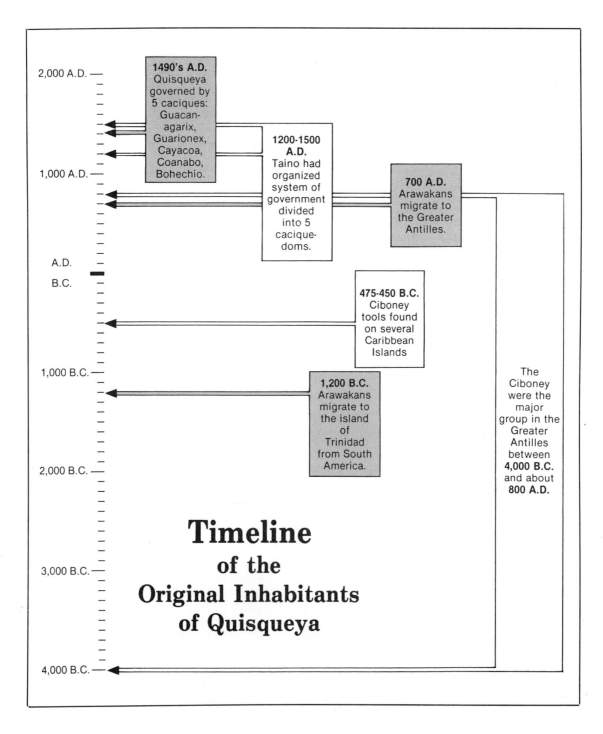

2,000 A.D. —

1490's A.D.
Quisqueya governed by 5 caciques: Guacan-agarix, Guarionex, Cayacoa, Coanabo, Bohechio.

1,000 A.D. —

1200-1500 A.D.
Taíno had organized system of government divided into 5 cacique-doms.

700 A.D.
Arawakans migrate to the Greater Antilles.

A.D. —

B.C. —

475-450 B.C.
Ciboney tools found on several Caribbean Islands

1,000 B.C. —

1,200 B.C.
Arawakans migrate to the island of Trinidad from South America.

The Ciboney were the major group in the Greater Antilles between **4,000 B.C.** and about **800 A.D.**

2,000 B.C. —

Timeline
of the
Original Inhabitants
of Quisqueya

3,000 B.C. —

4,000 B.C. —

The Dominican Republic is on an island located between Cuba and Puerto Rico. This island is the second largest island in the Caribbean. (See map on the following page.) It has had at least three other names in its history: Quisqueya (Kis-KAY-yah), Haití, and Hispaniola. It was named Quisqueya and Haití by early inhabitants more than 700 years ago.

The largest group of islands in the Caribbean is called the Greater Antilles. Quisqueya (shared today by the Dominican Republic and Haití), Cuba, Puerto Rico, and Jamaica make up this group of islands. (See map on the following page.) The earliest known people of the Greater Antilles were the Ciboney (Si-bo-NAY). Archaeologists and anthropologists have studied objects left behind by these early people in order to learn about their culture.[1] They have used the Carbon-14 dating process to decide the age of these objects.[2] From this research, they believe that, as long ago as 4,000 B.C., the Ciboney were the major group of people in the Greater Antilles.

By 700 A.D., another group of people called the Taíno-Arawak (Tah-EE-no A-rah-wahk) had migrated to the Greater Antilles. During the next 800 years, they developed their culture on Quisqueya and other islands in the Caribbean. They organized governments and a society based on the shared work of the community. The Taíno of Quisqueya were farmers, fishermen, hunters, and pottery makers. Religion was an important part of their daily life.

The Ciboney

The Ciboney lived on the part of the island which today is called the Dominican Republic. They hunted, fished, gathered food, and made stone tools such as flint knives, daggers, and stone axes. Because they used stone tools, it is said that they lived in a stone-age culture.[3] Their tools have been found on other Caribbean islands as far away as Trinidad, and date back to 475-450 B.C. Because of these findings, some

---

[1] Archaeologists study the objects left by people who lived in past times. Anthropologists study the origins, cultures, beliefs, and customs of people.

[2] The Carbon-14 dating process is done by measuring the amount of radioactivity coming from the carbon in an object, plant, or animal.

[3] Culture is the total way of life of a people. It includes the results of people's ideas and values, as seen in what they have produced over many centuries.

scientists think that the people of the Antilles traveled from island to island and traded with each other more than 2,400 years ago.

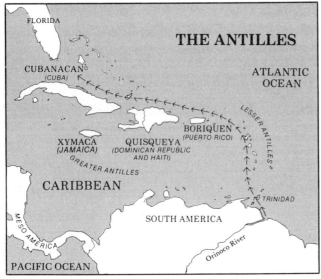

The arrow lines (→ → →) show the route of the Arawakan migration between 1200 B.C. and 700 A.D.

The Arawakan Migration

About 1200 B.C., a group of people who spoke the Arawakan language migrated to the island of Trinidad. It is thought that they came from the Orinoco (O-ree-no-koe) region in South America. (See map on this page.) Some of these people traveled north through the Lesser Antilles.[4] By 700 A.D., the Arawakan speaking people began migrating westward to the Greater Antilles. They settled on islands such as Boriquén (today called Puerto Rico) and Quisqueya (made up of the two countries today called Dominican Republic and Haití). Quisqueya means "mother of all lands" and Haití means "mountainous land." The culture of these early inhabitants was known as the Taíno culture.

Taíno Culture

Most of the Taíno were farmers whose main crops were maize and yucca. "Maize" was the Taíno word for corn. Yucca is a hard root vegetable used to make cassava bread and other cooked food.[5] The Taíno also fished and hunted. They built canoes, and made

Taíno pottery vase

fishing nets and hammocks from cotton. They were also skilled pottery makers. Taíno women made useful objects such as bowls, vases, and beads from clay and sea conch.

---

4 The Lesser Antilles are made up of more than two dozen small islands. These islands stretch from the Bahamas (south of Florida) to the northern part of Venezuela. Some of these islands are Trinidad, Barbados, Antigua, St. Thomas, St. Croix, and Aruba.

5 Cassava is a starch made from grated yucca.

This home of the cacique is called a bohío.

In addition to farming, fishing, hunting, and pottery making, the early inhabitants of Quisqueya spent time building their homes. These homes had two different shapes. One was circular with a cone-shaped roof. It was large enough for several families, and it was called a caney (kah-NAY-e). The other type of home was called a bohío (bo-EE-o) and was built for chiefs. It was rectangular, with a porch and a triangular roof. Taíno homes were made out of planks or cane, and thatched with palm leaves.

Communal Living

The Taíno had a *communal* society. This means that they believed in cooperation and equality for all members of the community. For example, all food grown was shared by everyone. Since yucca was a main food staple, it became the basis for the survival and growth of the Taíno people.

The Taíno used a barter system. They would meet at a central place for trade fairs at which they exchanged food, beads, gold nuggets, fish hooks, and tools. These trade fairs were very important to the economic life of the Taíno. The people of Quisqueya often traveled to other

Stone tools were used by the Taíno for bartering at trade fairs.

islands in the Caribbean to trade. Some of the things they traded were sea conch, salt, and cotton.

Religion

The Taíno believed in gods and goddesses who had power over the sea, the tides, the spring, the moon, and childbirth. Chanting and dancing were a part of Taíno religious celebrations. Healing was another part of religion. Healers were called behíques (bay-ee-kays). They used herbal plants, fruit, and tree leaves to make medicine. The behíques carried cemís (ce-MEE-s) with them. Cemís were objects made of wood, stone, clay, gold, and other materials, and had animal or human forms. It was believed that each cemí had power to heal the sick.

Taíno Government

Between 1200 A.D. and 1500 A.D., the Taíno people of Quisqueya (also called Haití at this time) had organized governments. The island was divided into five kingdoms or caciquedoms. Each caciquedom was governed by a chief. The chiefs were called caciques (kah-SEE-kays). The caciques had great power in all areas of community life, and were highly respected.

The chart below matches each cacique with his caciquedom. In Chapter 2, we will find out more about the caciquedoms. We will also learn about events which would cause major changes on the island of Quisqueya.

CACIQUES AND CACIQUEDOMS IN THE LATE 1400's

NAME OF CACIQUE	CACIQUEDOM
GUACANAGARIX (Goo-ah-kah-nah-gah-REEX)	MARIEN (Mah-RE-n)
GUARIONEX (Goo-ah-reeo-NEX)	MAGUA (MAH-goo-ah)
CAYACOA (Kah-yah-KO-ah)	HIGÜEY (E-goo-A)
CAONABO (Kah-oh-NAH-boh)	MAGUANA (Mah-goo-AH-nah)
BOHECHIO (Boh-ay-CHEE-oh)	JARAGUA (Hah-RAH-goo-ah)

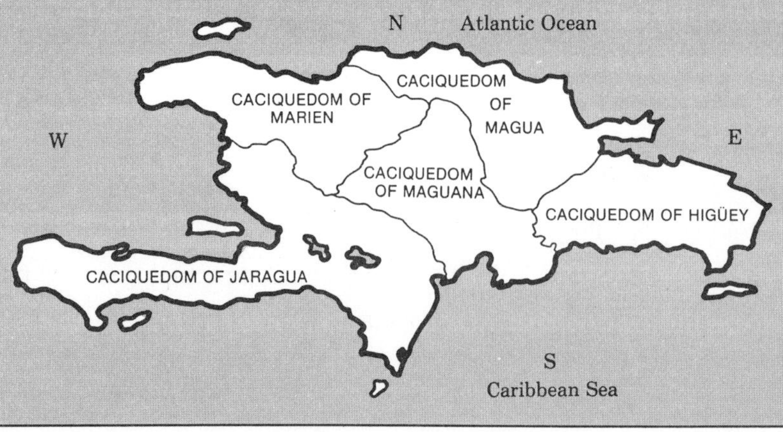

6

CHAPTER 1 REVIEW

I. **Vocabulary for Review**

   A. First, put the following words in alphabetical order. Then, using the glossary at the end of the book and a dictionary, write definitions for each word:

      dominant, migrate, inhabitants, staple, survival, barter, conch

   B. Use each word in a sentence of your own. Be sure to provide good context clues for the vocabulary word.

II. **Lesson Review**

   1. Which Caribbean islands form the Greater Antilles?

   2. Name two groups of original inhabitants who lived in the country we call the Dominican Republic today.

   3. Describe several aspects of Taíno culture on Quisqueya after 700 A.D.

   4. What role did the behíque play in Taíno society?

   5. What is a barter system? How was a barter system used by the Taíno of Quisqueya?

   6. List the five caciquedoms that existed on Quisqueya in the late 1400's.

III: **Enrichment Exercise**

   A. Copy the time line on page 2 of this chapter. Try to find pictures, or draw pictures of your own, to illustrate some of the important events and/or people mentioned on this time line.

   B. Choose several historical events of the last 20 years. Draw a time line that lists these events. Also include major events from your life, such as your date of birth. Use photographs, clippings from newspapers, or your own drawings to illustrate your time line.

CHAPTER

2

Christopher Columbus Brings Spanish Rule to the Americas

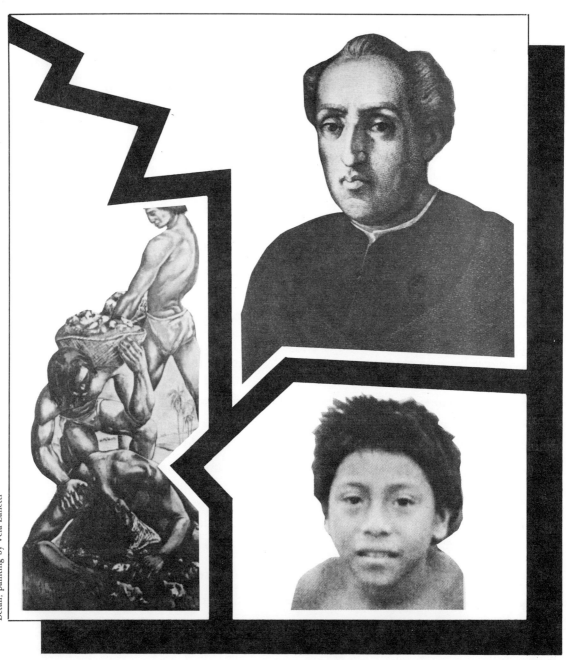

Detail, painting by Vela Zanetti

History is a description of the past. Some history books describe the arrival of Christopher Columbus in the Americas as a discovery. These books mention briefly that people were living in the Americas when Columbus arrived. Other history books explain that hundreds of cultures, with long traditions of achievement, existed in the Americas thousands of years before Columbus arrived. These books show events from the view of the original inhabitants. In these accounts, the arrival of Columbus and the following colonial period was an invasion, an attack on the cultures of the original inhabitants.

No matter how we describe the arrival of explorers and settlers, we do know that their coming brought about tremendous change. When Columbus and his men arrived on Quisqueya, they found the people and culture of the Taíno. At first, gifts were exchanged and the Spaniards learned about the lifestyle of the Taíno. When Columbus returned to Spain, the news of his voyage created great interest and support for more exploration.

Conflict between the Taíno and Spaniards on Quisqueya began when the Spaniards who stayed on the island abused Taíno men, women, and children. In the years that followed, Spaniards tried to force Taíno people to work as slaves. The Taíno organized many revolts and attempts to gain freedom. However, within fifty years, the original Taíno culture was destroyed.

The Search For A Shorter Water Route

Christopher Columbus was born in Genoa, Italy, in 1451.[1] While he was in his early twenties, Columbus learned how to navigate. He sailed around the Mediterranean Sea and the western coast of Africa.

Columbus wanted to sail to Japan, China, and India. In that time, Europeans called those countries the Indies. Columbus had an idea that he could find a shorter water route to the Indies by sailing west, even though the Indies were located east of Europe. He thought this because he believed that the world was round. In the late 1400's, many people in Europe did not believe that this theory was true.

---

[1] In Italian, Christopher Columbus is "Cristóforo Colombo." In Spanish, his name is "Cristóbal Colón."

Columbus decided to ask for help to carry out his plans. Since he was living in Portugal, which was the center of navigation and ship building in western Europe, he asked the king of Portugal, John II, to pay for his voyage. The king turned him down.

In 1485, Columbus moved to Spain. At this time, European merchants were trading with Asian merchants, and wanted to find a shorter water route to Asia. In this way, they could more easily get gold and spices from that part of the world. Columbus asked some of these wealthy merchants to pay for his expedition, but they were doubtful of Columbus' plan. There was one man, however, who thought that the plan might work. He was the Duke of Medinacelli. He decided to pay for the trip because he hoped that Columbus would find a new route to Asia. The duke paid for three ships to be built. He also agreed to provide all the supplies for the trip.

Queen Isabella of Spain

King Ferdinand of Spain

Columbus had asked the Spanish monarchs, Queen Isabella and King Ferdinand, for help on many occasions. They turned him down several times. In January of 1492, however, Queen Isabella finally decided to help Columbus. She used money from her treasury to repay the duke, and ordered the work on the ships to continue. After learning about the Queen's decision, Columbus went to the town of Palos in Spain. There he sought help from Martín Alonso Pinzón and his brother Vicente. They were well trained sailors, and Columbus wanted their help on the voyage. The Pinzón brothers agreed to help Columbus.

The First Voyage of Columbus

On August 3, 1492, Christopher Columbus sailed from the port of Palos in Spain. He was captain of the ship called La Santa María. There were two smaller ships called La Pinta and La Niña. The Pinzón brothers were captains of these two ships.

The captain of the Niña (above) was Vicente Yáñez Pinzón.

Columbus took a crew of 90 men on his first voyage. The map on page 20 and the detail map below show the route they sailed. After stopping at the Canary Islands off the coast of West Africa, the three ships headed west out into the Atlantic Ocean on September 9. On October 12, after more than one month at sea, they landed on an island in the Bahamas. Columbus called the island San Salvador. He thought that he had reached India. On October 28, Columbus landed on another island, which is today called Cuba.

Arrival on Quisqueya

On December 5, Columbus arrived on the island of Quisqueya. Since Columbus thought he was near the coast of India, he made the mistake of calling the original people living on Quisqueya and other islands "Indians."[2] Since then, the term "Indian" has been used to name the original people of the Americas.

Columbus landed on the north-western coast of the caciquedom

The route of Columbus on his first voyage.

of Marién. (See map, p. 6.) He had brought with him people who were from other islands where he had stopped. Some of these people had been kidnapped by Columbus. Others had agreed to come. These people spoke the Arawakan language and had also learned some Spanish. Columbus used them as interpreters who could communicate with the people of each island on which he landed.

A few days after Columbus landed on Quisqueya, he gave the island the name La Española. This was later changed to Hispaniola. By claiming and renaming Quisqueya, Columbus did not respect the original people's right to name and control their own land.

---

[2] The term "Indian" is not what people of Quisqueya called themselves. This name was given to them by the Spaniards. The early people on Quisqueya called themselves Ciboney and Taíno.

The Taíno and Spaniards Meet

After landing, Columbus sent three sailors to explore the island. The sailors saw many people, but the people would not come near them. The sailors were able to capture one woman. They took her to the ship. Columbus wrote the following in his log:

> She was very beautiful . . . and she talked with the other Indians on the ship . . . . They all spoke the same language. The admiral gave her clothing and items made out of glass, bells, a tin ring of no special value . . . . She was wearing a piece of gold pierced in her nose . . . a sign of the existence of gold on the island.[3]

Columbus wanted to find more gold. He sent this woman to her people with nine soldiers and an interpreter. On the island they saw thousands of houses, and more than a thousand men. The interpreter set up a meeting between the people of Marién and the Spaniards. Columbus thought that the local people were afraid. He told the interpreter to explain that there was nothing to fear. As soon as this was done, the people went to their homes and brought food for the sailors. They offered them cassava bread, fish, and whatever else they had. They also brought a parrot for Columbus. Columbus wrote this in his log:

> They gave anything they had, expecting nothing in return. They gave freely. They had no arms [weapons] . . . . They were handsome men and beautiful women . . . .

Finally, Columbus met Guacanagarix, the cacique (or king) of Marién. Columbus saw a large piece of gold around the cacique's neck. Because he wanted to find the source of gold on the island, he decided to be friendly to the cacique. Perhaps Guacanagarix would tell him where to find the gold. Columbus was given many gifts of gold. He wrote:

> They also gave pieces of gold the same way they gave water in bottle shaped gourds. How easy it is to recognize when you give something with all your heart.

It was hard for Columbus to understand why people would give gold so freely. He thought that gold was something to be sold. People from Europe thought of gold in that way. Owning gold was a way to become wealthy and powerful. In Europe, only rich people had gold. On Quisqueya, everyone had some gold. It was used to make religious objects, sculptures, and decorations.

---

[3] A log is a record of events kept by the captain of a ship.

Columbus sails back to Spain.

Columbus Returns to Spain

Before Columbus left Quisqueya, he exchanged gifts with the cacique of Marién. He also built a fort on the island and left thirty nine people there. Among those who stayed were a carpenter, officers to keep the peace, a clerk, a shipwright (ship builder), a tailor, a cooper (barrel maker), and a medic.

Columbus left Quisqueya on January 2, 1493, and arrived in Spain on March 15, 1493. He was awarded great honors in Spain. The king and queen granted Columbus three titles. He was now called Admiral of the Ocean, Viceroy, and Governor. People in Spain and Portugal thought that Columbus had found a shorter water route to the Indies.

Conflicts Between Spain and Portugal

Soon, conflicts arose between Spain and Portugal. Each country wanted to claim and take control of land in the Americas.[4] The leaders of each country asked Pope Alexander VI to decide which lands they could claim and take. The Pope drew an imaginary line which ran from north to south. This line was about 350 miles west of the Azores Islands. (See map on this page.) It was called the Line of Demarcation. The Pope said that all non-Christian lands east of this line could be taken by Portugal. All non-Christian lands west of the line could be taken by Spain. The

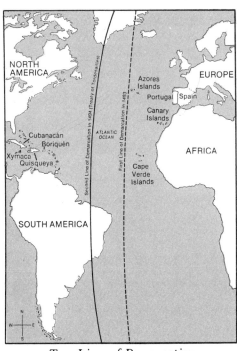

Two Lines of Demarcation.

Portuguese leaders were not satisfied, and said that this decision favored Spain. One year later, the Pope moved the line so that it fell 1,295 miles to the west of Cape Verde Islands. This new imaginary line ran through what is known as South America today. The agreement drawn up by the Pope was called the Treaty of Tordesailles.

---

4 At this time in history, Europeans thought that they had the right to claim and take the land of people who were not Christian. In the Caribbean, this belief led to the destruction of the original inhabitants' cultures. It also led to the control and colonization of the Americas by several European countries.

The Second Voyage of Christopher Columbus

In 1493, the king and queen of Spain sent Christopher Columbus on a second voyage. They agreed to do this because of the success of his first voyage. This time, Columbus had seventeen ships and at least 1,300 men. Among the crew were land-owners, artisans, soldiers, and priests. Columbus was sent to find gold, to claim more land, and to dominate the people who lived there. The king and queen wanted Columbus to begin converting people to Christianity. They also hoped that Columbus would find the kingdoms of Japan and China.

When Columbus reached the Caribbean, he landed on many of the islands known as the Lesser Antilles today.[5] He also landed on the island of Boriquén, which is called Puerto Rico today.

Columbus arrived on Quisqueya for the second time on November 28, 1493. Caci-que Guacanagarix, Columbus' friend, told him that the thirty nine Spaniards left on the island had been killed. These men had abused many of the women on the island. Because of this, another cacique, named Caonabo of Maguana, had burned down the Spanish fort. He and his men had killed all the Spaniards. This event was the begin-ning of struggle against European colonization of the island of Quisqueya.

Colonial Settlement Begins

Columbus decided to build a colonial settlement on Quisqueya. He ordered three hundred of his men to build a city. He named the city "Isabella" in honor of the queen of Spain. He also had a fort called Santo Tomás built in the kingdom of Maguana.

Christopher Columbus left his brother Diego in charge of the city of Isabella while he went to explore the coast of Cuba. Before he left, he assigned work to his men. For instance, they were to build their own homes and plant their own crops.

While Columbus was gone, many of his men became very angry and rebelled against Diego Columbus. They felt that Diego Columbus was punishing them by making them work under hard conditions. Many of these men had been rich land-owners in Spain. Because they were not used to hard work, some became sick, others died, and some returned to Spain.

In order to continue the hard work of building a colony, the remaining Spaniards

---

[5] Some of the islands in the Lesser Antilles are Guadalupe, Antigua, Monserrate, Nevis, St. Croix, and the Virgin Islands.

decided to force the Taíno to work as slaves. The Taíno were forced to grow food, and to build roads, homes, and towns. Those Taíno who resisted were beaten, tortured, or killed.

Columbus Orders An Attack on the Taíno

When Columbus returned to Quisqueya, he learned that Cacique Caonabo and his men were leaving their villages and getting ready to fight the Spaniards again. They were preparing to attack Fort St. Tomás. Columbus sent seventy men with arms and food to St. Tomás. He told these men to spread terror among the people on their way to the fort. He wanted to show how strong and powerful the Christians were. Guns, dogs, and horses were used to terrorize the people.

In 1495, Cacique Caonabo was captured. He was sent off to Spain, but died on the ship before it reached Europe. Other caciques were captured and chained. Women were abused. People were beaten and murdered. Still, the Taíno continued to revolt against Spanish colonization.

Taíno were tortured and murdered by the Spaniards.

BARTOLOME COLUMBUS

Struggle for Power Among the Spaniards

When Columbus returned to Spain in 1496, he left another brother, Bartolomé, in charge as the governor of the island. A man named Francisco Roldán was the mayor of Isabella. Roldán did not get along with Bartolomé, and led a rebellion against the governor. Some Taíno joined Roldán's rebellion when he promised them better treatment. Together, they attacked and burned the original city of Isabella.

After this, Bartolomé decided to move the city of Isabella to the southern part of the island, because gold had been found there and because of conflicts with Roldán. He moved the city across the Ozama River that same year, and changed its name to Santo Domingo de Guzmán. Today, this city is the capital of the Dominican Republic.

Arrival of Francisco de Bobadilla.

In 1498, Christopher Columbus returned to Quisqueya for the third time. Because the island was in turmoil, the king and queen of Spain sent a new governor to Quisqueya in 1500. His name was Francisco de Bobadilla. He was an enemy of Columbus and his brothers. When he arrived on the island, he arrested Columbus and his brothers and sent them in chains to Spain. Two years passed before Columbus was able to get out of prison and return to the island.

Attacks Against the Taíno Continue

When Columbus returned on his fourth trip in 1502, the Taíno had been fighting for eight years against the brutality of the Spaniards. The governor of Quisqueya, Nicolás de Ovando, had taken harsh measures against the people of the island. Caciques were being hanged. Many other people were murdered.

One of the last caciques on the island was Anacaona, cacica of Jaragua. (See map on p. 6.)[6] Ovando had heard that Cacica Anacaona was plotting against him. He sent almost four hundred men to Juaragua. These men were welcomed by Anacaona, who did not know what Ovando had told his men to do. While the Spaniards were putting on a military display for Anacaona and her people, the soldiers opened fire on the crowd, killing men, women, and children. Cacica Anacaona was captured, taken to Santo Domingo, and hanged. Those who were not killed were forced to work as slaves.

Nicolás de Ovando

Cacica Anacaona

Ovando continued to kill Taíno by the thousands. Some escaped to neighboring islands. Others took cassava poison rather than live under Spanish rule. By 1504, the revolt begun by Caonabo had ended.

Over time, the rule of the Spaniards destroyed the communal lifestyle of the Taíno

---

[6] "Cacica" is the female form of "cacique." It is used to refer to a woman who governs a caciquedom (kingdom).

people of Quisqueya. It was replaced by a form of slavery and control called "reparti-miento" (reh-par-ti-me-EN-tow). Under "repartimiento," Spaniards took control of the land and the people on the land. They were very cruel to the Taíno, and forced them to work long hours under brutal conditions. When the king and queen of Spain found out about this brutal treatment, they brought about a new system called "enco-mienda" (en-co-me-EN-dah). In this system, the Spaniards still controlled the land and the people. They tried to convince the Taíno to follow the Roman Catholic religion. Also, they were supposed to take better care of the Taíno. This did not happen. The local people were still forced to work as slaves. The caciquedoms that Columbus had found when he arrived in 1492 were destroyed. As the Spanish invaders colonized Quisqueya, they violently disrupted the people's way of life. Although the people resisted, they were overpowered.

Bartolomé de las Casas

Defender of the Taíno

Bartolomé de Las Casas was a Spanish landowner who had come with Columbus. During his first years on Quisqueya he was given an "encomienda" (plantation) and "owned" many Taíno.[7] In 1510, Las Casas became a priest. He began to speak out against the Spaniards' cruel treatment of the Taíno. Because of this treatment, he said, the Taíno would connect Christianity with terror. Las Casas kept a written record of what happened to the Taíno during the colonization of Quisqueya by the Spaniards. His most well-known writing is a book called *History of the Indies*.

Result of Colonization for the Taíno People

Archaeologists have estimated that there were between three hundred thousand and three million people living on Quisqueya when the Spaniards arrived in 1492. Four years later, one third of these people had been killed by soldiers, or had died of starvation and disease brought by the Spaniards.[8] Others died from the brutal treatment of slavery, or took cassava poison to avoid these horrors. Those who fled to other places often faced a similar fate. A census taken in 1508 counted about sixty thousand Taíno people on Quisqueya. Forty years later, only five hundred Taíno were still alive.

---

[7] Quotation marks are placed around the word "owned" because no person can really own another.

[8] The people of Quisqueya died of diseases brought by the Spaniards because they had no resistance to these diseases, which were new to them.

CHAPTER 2 REVIEW

I. Vocabulary for Review

A. First, put the following words in alphabetical order. Then, using the glossary at the end of the book and a dictionary, write definitions for each word:

> invasion, tremendous, navigate, voyage, expedition, monarch, imaginary, artisans, convert, rebel, terrorize, brutal, communal, turmoil, colonization

B. Use each word in a sentence of your own. Be sure to provide good context clues for the vocabulary word.

II. Lesson Review

1. Who was the first person to agree to pay for Christopher Columbus' trip?

2. Describe the relationship that Cacique Caonabo and Cacica Anacaona had with the Spaniards.

3. Why did Bartolomé Columbus move the city of Isabella and change its name?

4. In what ways did the Spaniards destroy the Taíno way of life during the period of colonization?

III. Critical Thinking and Writing

A. Many books state that "Columbus discovered America." Write a paragraph explaining how this statement could be seen as both true and false. In your explanation, look at the statement from both a Taíno and a Spanish point of view.

B. Spaniards colonized many of the islands in the Caribbean. There was a similar pattern of colonization on each island. Use another book in this series (such as **Puerto Rico** or **Cuba**) to compare colonization on Quisqueya to colonization on one of these islands.

IV. Enrichment

Read again the information in your text on Cacica Anacaona. Make one or more drawings which portray this information. Use pictures in Chapters 1 and 2 for ideas about what people and places of the early 1500's looked like.

WHEN DID AFRICAN PEOPLE COME TO THE AMERICAS?*

Some scientists and historians believe that African sailors, merchants and explorers came to the Americas before Columbus and other European explorers. There are also linguists who think that very early contact took place between African and Caribbean peoples.[1] They point to studies which have compared the languages of the Taíno (Caribbean) and the Mandinka (West Africa). These studies have found common words in the languages of the two regions.

Language Links

Similarities between languages are one way to show that contact may have existed between different cultural groups. In the Caribbean, the Taíno word "nitaíno" means noble man or leader. In the Mande language of the Mandinka, this word has the same meaning. In several

LANGUAGE COMPARISONS

Caribbean	West African	English
Goana, Caona, Guani, Guanín	Ghana, Kane, Kani, Ghanin	Gold
Nucay, Nozay	Néǵǵ, nexe	Metal: Iron, or Gold Jewelry
bo- (bohío)	bö	House
Caonabo (Name of a Cacique in Haití)	Kane-bö	House of Gold
Tuob, Tumbaga	Sabu Tubab, Tobauto Mansa Tobauto Mansa	Gold, A Gold Weight, A King's Title
Caracole	Caragole	A Point of Land in Southwest Panamá A Branch of the Mandinka Nation
Nitaíno	Nitaíno	Noble Man or Leader

*(The information in this chart is from the research of Harold G. Lawrence, in **African Presence in Early America**.)*

Caribbean islands, the gold breastplate of the cacique (king) is called a "guanín."[2] In West African languages, "ghanin" is the plural form of "quanin" and means gold. Another form of the same word is "Ghana," which was the name of a West African empire of the Middle Ages known for its wealth in gold. The chart on this page shows a few comparisons between words used in Caribbean languages and words used in West African languages. When this information is combined with other evidence, the case for a very early African presence in the Americas becomes even stronger.

---

* This vignette was contributed by Ellen Swartz, Project Coordinator.

1 Linguists are experts in the origin and development of languages. They also study the relationships among languages.

2 The breastplate was a large disc made of gold, worn on the chest of a cacique as a symbol of power.

What Had Columbus Learned?

On Columbus' third voyage to the Americas (1498), he stopped at one of the Cape Verde Islands to get supplies. (See map below.) This island was more than three hundred miles west of Africa. Columbus was told by people who lived there that West African canoes carrying goods for sale had been seen traveling westward, near an island more than fifty miles to the southwest.

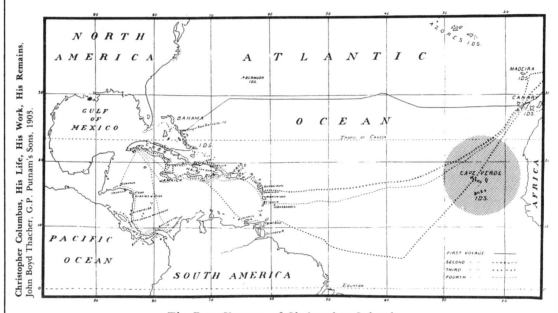

The Four Voyages of Christopher Columbus

Christopher Columbus, His Life, His Work, His Remains, John Boyd Thacher, G.P. Putnam's Sons, 1903.

Columbus was already aware of the boat building and navigating skills of West Africans. Portuguese sailors had traveled to West Africa for many years and had brought this information back to Europe. Columbus may have wondered if there was a connection between these West African merchant sailors and people described to his men by the inhabitants of Hispaniola. His men were told ". . . that there had come to Espanola from the south and south-east, a black people who have the tops of their spears made of a metal which they call 'guanín'." [3] Could these visitors have come from South America? Columbus sent samples of this metal to Spain to be tested, and it was found to be made of eighteen parts gold, six parts silver, and eight parts

---

[3] John Boyd Thacher, **Christopher Columbus, His Life, His Work, His Remains**, vol. II, p. 380 (1903). Thacher's account of Columbus' voyages is taken largely from three sources: two works by Bartolomé de Las Casas and a work by Ferdinand Columbus. The Las Casas works are: 1) the abridged version of Columbus' original **Journal**, which is now lost, published in 1825 by Martin Fernández de Navarrete; and 2) **Historia de las Indias**, completed in 1559 and first printed in 1877. Ferdinand Columbus' book is entitled **Historie**, published in Italian in 1571.

copper. The process for alloying or blending these three metals in this way had been practiced for centuries in West Africa. Could these visitors who came to Hispaniola have been from West Africa? Is there any other evidence that points to an early African presence in the Americas?

Other Findings

Many sculptures that portray African people have been found at sites in México. Also, skeletons of African people have been uncovered in several places in the Caribbean. By using a method called carbon-14 dating, scientists have shown that some of these findings date back as far as 1000 B.C.[4]

The clay head (below) dates to the 1300's A.D. and is a likeness of a Man-

*Mandinka head
from the 1300's, México*

dinka. The ear pendants are like those worn by the Mandinka in West Africa during the same time period. This sculpture was found in the Oaxaca region of México, where the Mixtec culture was located. Another sculpture which depicts Mandinka boatmen has been found in the same region. This sculpture also dates to the 1300's A.D. It was made about the same time that two Mandinka ocean voyages occurred.

Mandinka Voyages

Written records tell us that Emperor Abubakar II of Mali sent a fleet of four hundred ships to explore the Atlantic Ocean in 1307. (See map on the following page.) He told the sailors "to explore the limits of the neighboring sea." Only one ship returned. The captain of this ship said that the other ships, which were ahead of his, had run into a strong current and disappeared. They did not come back, and he returned to Africa.

---

4 See page 3, footnote no. 2.

Abubakar II decided to lead a second exploration himself. He left the west coast of Africa with a fleet of two thousand large and small ships. His fleet had a large crew and was well stocked with food, water, gold, and other supplies for a long voyage.

Abubakar thought that, by sailing westward on the ocean, he might find another land. He left his brother Mansa Musa in charge, and was never again seen in Mali.

Is it possible that the fleets of Abubakar II landed in México? It is known that strong, underwater currents flow between the west coast of Africa and the east coast of the Americas. (See map below.) Did these strong currents pull the ships of both Mandinka fleets to the Americas?

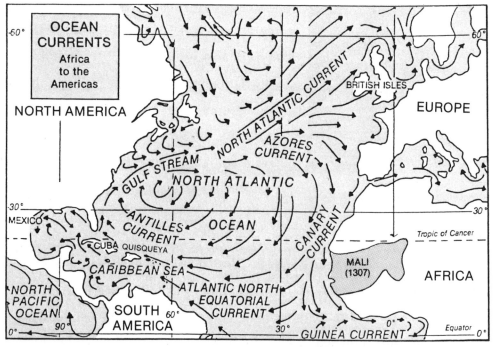

The Canary Current and the Atlantic North Equatorial Current carry ships from the west coast of Africa to the Americas.

Thor Heyerdahl's boat, Ra I

Current Research

In 1969, a Norwegian writer and explorer sailed from the west coast of Africa to the Caribbean. His boat, Ra I, was made of papyrus (a stiff grass-like plant) and built by African boat builders in the late 1960's. It was designed and built like ancient Egyptian boats. Soon after he began his journey, the rudders on the boat broke. He could no longer steer, and the ocean currents carried him westward until he arrived in the Caribbean. This drift journey shows that it could have been possible for African sailors to come to the Americas centuries before on these same ocean currents. Thor Heyerdahl's voyage was only one of more than one hundred recorded experiments which show that African sailors could have crossed the Atlantic before Columbus and other European explorers.

As scientists, historians, and linguists continue to conduct research on early African travelers, we may learn more about the presence of Africans in the Americas. In this way, history is alive, because new information keeps shaping and changing the way we look at the past.

CHAPTER

3

The Colonial Development of Hispaniola

Hispaniola was the main Spanish colony until the mid-1500's. Its city of Santo Domingo was the center of Spain's colonial governments in the Americas. By 1509, there were three gold mines on Hispaniola, and sugar cane was under production.

Spain controlled all trade with Hispaniola. On the second voyage of Christopher Columbus, the Spaniards brought horses, cattle, sheep, oranges, limes, rice, lemons, herbs, and many kinds of flowers. The colonists began to raise sheep, goats, horses, and donkeys.

Beginning in the mid-1500's, Hispaniola was invaded by other European nations. French invaders set up a colony on the western part of the island. As a result, the island was divided into two colonies: one Spanish, one French. Eventually, the French colony became known as Haití, and the Spanish colony became known as the Dominican Republic.

The Rule of Diego Columbus

In 1509, King Ferdinand of Spain appointed Christopher Columbus' son Diego to be the Viceroy, Admiral, and Governor of the island of Hispaniola. Diego Columbus ruled the colony for nine years, for a period of two terms. The first term was from 1509 to 1514, and the second was from 1520 to 1524. Diego Columbus built a governor's mansion, made plans for the building of a cathedral, and ordered Diego Velázquez to colonize Cuba. He also enforced the "encomienda" system. (See p. 17.)

Problems Arise

The first term of the governor was not smooth, and tensions among the ruling colonists resulted in conflicts. Some colonists who were loyal to King Ferdinand, said that Diego Columbus had taken too much authority, that some of his actions on Hispaniola were not approved by the king.

Rumors of the tension on the island traveled to the king. He set up a Supreme Tribunal, or Council, to handle disputes on the island. This weakened the authority of Diego Columbus, who returned to Spain in 1514.

In 1520, Diego Columbus returned to Hispaniola for a second term as governor. He was appointed by Charles V of Spain, four years after the death of King Ferdinand.

King Charles V of Spain

When he arrived, Columbus tried to end the colonist's dispute about who would control the island.

The Last Taíno Rebellion

During the second term of Diego Columbus, the last Taíno rebellion was taking place in the old Jaragua Caciquedom (1520). This rebellion was led by a cacique named Guarocuya (Goo-ah-ro-coo-yah; in Spanish, Enriquillo) (N-ree-KEY-yo). Enriquillo had been educated by Franciscan priests. He lived on one of the last encomiendas on Hispaniola. Enriquillo wanted to stop the attacks against his people by the Spaniards. For example, many Taíno women were abused and dishonored by Spanish men. Enriquillo's wife, Mencia, was one of these women.

In 1520, Enriquillo led the Taíno in a rebellion. Their base of operation was in the mountains. In 1522, they were joined by many enslaved Africans who also rebelled against the cruel treatment of the Spaniards. (See pp. 27-28.)

The colonial government could not control Enriquillo's rebellion. At the same time, Diego Columbus was unable to improve relationships among the colonists. He returned to Spain again in 1524 to present his case to King Charles V.

Dominican Republic stamp honors Enriquillo and Mencia.

In 1533, the king sent an envoy to negotiate a peace treaty with Cacique Enriquillo, whose rebellion had lasted thirteen years. As a result, between one thousand and four thousand enslaved Taíno were freed. However, despite this treaty, Spaniards continued to abuse the Taíno, and disease brought by the Spaniards killed the Taíno in large numbers. By 1550, almost none of the original people were left on Quisqueya.

Slavery Is Used to Develop Hispaniola

In 1503, before Diego Columbus became governor, a small group of African people were brought from Spain to Santo Domingo and enslaved.[1] However, these Africans revolted and escaped to the mountains to live. After this, the governor, Nicolás de Ovando, made a law that no Christian Spaniards of African descent could be brought to Hispaniola to work as slaves. Colonists who broke this law had to pay one thousand pesos, or receive one hundred lashes for their crime. By making this law, Ovando hoped to avoid future revolts. A few years later, the king of Spain changed this law.

After Diego Columbus became governor, the king of Spain ordered one hundred fifty Black Spaniards to be sent to Hispaniola in 1510. He also ordered Black women to be taken from Spain to Hispaniola, because he thought enslaved Black men would not revolt if these women were on the island. In addition, the king ordered white females from Spain to be taken to Santo Domingo and enslaved. He thought that white women would work harder than Taíno women. He also hoped that Spanish soldiers would marry these women, rather than the local women.

African people were forced to work in the gold mines and on sugar plantations.

While Diego Columbus was in Spain (1514-1520), the Jerónimo priests ruled the island.[2] At this time, the original inhabitants of the island (called Indians by the Spaniards) were dying in large numbers. A chicken pox epidemic broke out at this time and killed one fourth of their population. Because the Jerónimo priests wanted workers to replace these people, they were eager to bring more African people to Hispaniola and enslave them. They had learned that African people had many of the skills needed to develop their colonial economy.

---

[1] All trade to Spanish colonies was controlled by Spain. Because the king wanted to keep some of the profits from the slave trade, it was illegal to "buy" or "sell" people without permission and a special license.

[2] The Jerónimo priests were members of the Dominican order of priests.

The colonists used slavery to develop the sugar industry and to raise cattle. By the year 1527, there were twenty sugar plantations on the island. As the number of plantations grew, the enslaved population increased. Many colonists became wealthy by using the forced labor of African people.

Revolts Against Slavery

There were many slave revolts. If the leaders of these revolts were caught, they were either hanged or burned immediately. However, the colonial government of Hispaniola could not always prevent enslaved people from taking their freedom. These people often organized themselves in groups, and took refuge in mountains and caves on the island.

By 1568, approximately twenty thousand enslaved Africans and their descendants lived on Hispaniola. The system of slavery, upon which the economy of the colony was built, continued for more than two hundred years.

During the 1500's, enslaved Africans were forced to carry wealthy Spaniards in a vehicle called a litera.

Links Between Hispaniola and Europe

During the late 1500's, the colonists of Hispaniola wanted to trade with other European nations. They did not want Spain to control all trade with the island. When war broke out between Spain and France, Spain was unable to supply the colony with the products it needed, and many colonists made private deals with Portuguese, German, and Dutch merchants. The king of Spain did not approve of these private deals. To demonstrate his disapproval, he ordered his soldiers to seize all ships from other countries docked at Spanish ports. Despite the king's action, many colonists continued illegal trade with other countries. When the king decided to tax the sale of slaves and all goods traded on Hispaniola, the colonists became very upset. They wanted free trade with other European countries.

The Role of Pirates

In the last half of the 1500's, English, French, and Dutch pirates looted cities and towns in the Americas. Ship captains (called filibusters) were given money and supplies for their ships by these governments. Part of the loot that these pirates stole was then returned to the government that supported them.

Francis Drake was an English pirate who invaded the city of Santo Domingo in 1586. The governor and most of the people fled to the countryside, and Drake took over the city for thirty days. From his headquarters in the cathedral, he stole the church bell, gold, silver, jewels, hides, and sugar. Only when the governor paid Drake twenty five thousand ducats (Spanish currency) did Drake agree to leave Santo Domingo. Later, Dutch and French pirates also invaded Hispaniola to steal cattle.

Invasions and raids against Hispaniola continued for two centuries. In 1655, British troops attempted to take over the island, landing their ships southwest of the city of Santo Domingo. Spanish colonial troops fought the British and defeated them. A few decades later, the French also invaded Hispaniola.

French pirates often raided Spanish colonies during the 1500's.

Francis Drake, well-known English pirate.

The French Establish a Colony on Hispaniola

During the mid-1600's, the French were gaining influence on the western part of Hispaniola. They traded in tobacco, hides, and sugar. In 1673, French troops invaded the island from the east. After six years of fighting, France and Spain worked out a peace treaty. This temporary treaty allowed the French to establish a colony called St. Domingue on the western part of the island. (This part of the island is now called Haití). The founding of St. Domingue divided Hispaniola into two colonies —a French colony, and a Spanish colony.

The Development of St. Domingue

During the 1700's, St. Domingue became one of the wealthiest colonies in the Americas. This wealth was built largely with the labor and skills of enslaved people. The French gained full control, or monopoly, over the tobacco industry. They were also involved in the sugar industry. During the 1780's, the French supplied sugar, molasses, wood, and liquor to the newly independent United States.

Britain wanted to weaken the power of the French in the Antilles. One way in which the British tried to do this was by encouraging abolitionist groups to form on St. Domingue. They knew that ending the system of slavery would limit the power of the French.

French Colonial Society in St. Domingue

French colonial society was made up of three separate groups:

* The most powerful group were the French colonists, or rich white plantation owners. They wanted to form an independent country similar to the United States.

* People whose ancestors were both European and African were called mulattoes. They owned about one third of the property of St. Domingue.

* The third group of people in St. Domingue were enslaved Black people, who made up the majority in this French colony.

There was tension among these three groups. The enslaved Black majority sought freedom from white plantation owners. Mulattoes wanted economic and social equality with white plantation owners. Many Black and mulatto people in St. Domingue had heard about the French Revolution (1789), which was based on the ideals of freedom and equality. News of this Revolution helped fire their desire for equal rights.

The rich plantation owners had passed laws which discriminated against mulattoes. They feared mulatto property owners, because they did not want the descendants of slaves to have important positions in the colony. By passing these laws, plantation owners hoped to limit the economic, political, and social power of mulattoes. At the same time, some mulattoes did not support the abolition of slavery, even though they opposed the colonial system which tried to limit their own rights.

French colonists opposed freedom and equality for people of African descent. Without the slavery system, and without laws limiting the rights of free Black people, colonists would lose their wealth and power. The government of France, like the colonists, wanted to maintain the slave trade in order to keep its dominant place in the world market. Meanwhile, slave revolts continued into the 1790's.

Slave rebellion of 1791, St. Domingue.

The Bettman Archive

Fight for independence against French troops in St. Domingue.

Toussaint L'Ouverture: A Great Leader Fights for Freedom

Francois-Domingue Toussaint, known as Toussaint L'Ouverture, led a major slave rebellion in the western part of the island. This rebellion led to the Haitian Revolution. Toussaint was an inspiring leader who trained excellent soldiers. They won many battles against the troops of France, Spain, and England. Each of these countries wanted to control the western part of the island, but Toussaint was able to defeat all three and take control of the old French colony. In 1801, he abolished the system of slavery and began to build roads, bridges, schools, and buildings. He strengthened his army and improved farming.

The French general Napoleón Bonaparte wanted to overthrow Toussaint L'Ouverture and regain control of St. Domingue. Napoleón hoped to create a huge empire in the Western hemisphere, and Toussaint was in his way. He ordered a huge fleet with more than twenty five thousand men to crush Toussaint's revolution. After two years of heavy fighting, Toussaint was tricked when he agreed to meet with a French general. When he arrived for the meeting, he was kidnapped and sent to prison in France, where he died of starvation in 1803.

Toussaint L'Ouverture

Brown Brothers Stock Photos

Napoleón Bonaparte

Toussaint's men continued to fight French troops, who used terror and mass murder against Toussaint's followers. Jean-Jacques Dessalines, a general under Toussaint, took charge of the troops after Toussaint's capture. When he learned that Napoleón planned to bring the system of slavery back to the island, he challenged the French: "War for war, crime for crime, atrocity for atrocity." Dessalines kept his challenge and his word. On his orders, most of the white people left in St. Domingue were killed.

Dessalines finally defeated the French, and on January 1, 1804, the Republic of Haití was born. This was the first country in Latin America to become independent from colonial rule. Dessalines was appointed ruler of Haití by his military followers, and later declared himself emperor.

CHAPTER 3 REVIEW

I. **Vocabulary for Review**

   A. First, put the following words in alphabetical order. Then, using the glossary at the end of the book and a dictionary, write definitions for each word:

   > mansion, cathedral, tension, authority, negotiate, population, conflict, invasion, influence, abolitionist, discriminate.

   B. Use each word in a sentence of your own. Be sure to provide good context clues for the vocabulary word.

II. **Lesson Review**

   1. What city was considered the center of Spain's colonial government in the early 1500's?

   2. Name some of the plants and animals brought to Hispaniola by the Spaniards.

   3. What two independent countries are now on the island?

   4. Why did Cacique Enriquillo lead a rebellion against the Spaniards?

   5. What nations, other than Spain, invaded Hispaniola?

   6. Who led a revolt against slavery in St. Domingue?

   7. What was the first country in Latin America to become independent from colonial rule?

III. **Critical Thinking and Writing**

   A. Write a paragraph explaining how two separate colonies developed on the island of Hispaniola.

   B. The time is the late 1600's. You may choose to be one of the following: Taíno, African, Spaniard, French, English. From your point of view, which part of the island would you prefer to live on, and why?

IV. **Enrichment Exercise**

   Visit the school library or your neighborhood public library. Find out what you can about the Spanish Inquisition during the time of Columbus' journeys to the Americas. Report back to your class.

CHAPTER

Hispaniola:
One Country or Two?

Gonzalo Briones / Listín Diario

By the end of 1803, the Haitian Revolution was successful. The French were defeated and independence was won. Many changes took place on the island. The Haitian Constitution of 1801 proclaimed that the island was "indivisible." This meant that it could not be divided. The new Haitian leaders believed that it was their right to control the entire island. While the western part of the island was under Haitian control, the eastern part was under Spanish control. This changed when Haití took over the entire island in 1822. A new fight for independence from Haití led to the establishment of the Dominican Republic in 1844.

After Independence

After winning independence, Haitians decided to keep the Arawakan name "Haití" for their new republic. This republic was on the western side of the island. Most of the business life of Haití was conducted from the capital city, called Port-au-Prince. Haitians spoke Créole and French.[1] The people living on the eastern part of the island spoke Spanish and remained under Spanish rule. Most of the business life of the Spanish colony was conducted from the city called Santo Domingo.

Richard A. Meek

Jean-Jacques Dessalines was assassinated in 1806, and one year later Henri Christophe became the President of Haití. He had fought with Toussaint L'Ouverture against the French, and had served as a general under Jean-Jacques Dessalines.

Christophe is known for having built a huge fortress to guard against a French invasion. Thousands of lives were lost in the building of this fortress. Christophe also made harsh labor laws in order to rebuild the country after the Haitian Revolution. Workers on plantations had to toil from daybreak to evening. People who were caught idle or begging were severely punished.

---

[1] Créole is a language which developed as a result of contact in the 1500's between French sailors/traders and the people of West Africa. Créole is a non-standard form of the French language combined with the languages of African people. Today, both Créole and French are spoken in Haití. Créole is spoken by the majority of people. However, French is the language used in schools, courts, and government offices.

French Try to Control the Spanish Colony

After the Haitian Revolution, some French officials and soldiers fled to Santo Domingo and settled there. They did not think they would be safe in Haití. At that time, the Spanish colony on Hispaniola was very weak and the newly arrived French began a war to take control. As they received food and supplies from French ships, they increased their strength.

The Spanish governor of Santo Domingo asked England for help in removing the French. England agreed, and set up a blockade in the port of Santo Domingo. This blockade prevented French ships from bringing food and supplies to French soldiers. Without this help, the French were defeated in a war that was followed by a period of misery and hunger. In order to survive, citizens and soldiers were forced to eat horse meat, burros, rats, pigeons, and parrots. Some people even ate boiled cattle hides. There was almost no commercial agriculture, mining, or production of goods during this time.

Spain Takes Back Some Control

At this time, Spain faced her own economic and military problems in Europe. Because of these problems, Spain had not paid much attention to her colony on Hispaniola. There were some people in Santo Domingo who wanted Spain to become a strong force again in the colony. Spain agreed to send new troops to Hispaniola to take back some control. This period of Spanish control lasted until 1821. During this period, Spain tried to develop agriculture on the island. However, this attempt did not meet with much success.

Haitian Control: 1822-1844

When Jean Pierre Boyer became the president of Haití in 1818, he promised to give land to his followers. In order to keep this promise, he developed a plan by which the Republic of Haití could control the entire island. Boyer sent men to Santo Domingo and other cities in the Spanish colony. Their mission was to persuade the Spanish speaking inhabitants to become part of Haití. Boyer's men promised land and freedom to those who agreed to become a part of Haití.

By 1821, there were three groups or political parties in the Spanish colony. Each group had a different goal. Boyer's group was in favor of Haitian control. Another group was in favor of independence, and still another wanted Spain to remain in control of the colony. On December 1, 1821, the independence group declared an "Independent State of Spanish Haití." This state was to be under the protection of Colombia, which also included the territories of Panama, Venezuela, and Equador. The new state of Spanish Haití lasted only two months.

On February 9, 1822, President Boyer invaded the Spanish colony with twelve thousand soldiers. He was successful in this invasion because the colony's army was very weak. The Spanish governor, Núñez de Cáceres, handed control to President Boyer. The eastern or Spanish part of the island was now under the laws of the Republic of Haití.

Sugar cane field

Agriculture and Trade

The Haitian government tried to develop agriculture on the eastern part of the island. The production of coffee, cocoa, cotton, and fruit was increased. However, people were not very interested in this type of agriculture. Cattle raising, sugar milling, and tobacco growing had been the main economic activities in the former Spanish colony.

At this time, foreign countries were interested in buying tobacco and wood from Haití. However, because he wanted to protect Haití from foreign influence, Boyer captured all ships entering ports on the island. Only Dutch ships were allowed to do business with Haití. President Boyer trusted the Dutch because they showed an interest in trading, not in dominating the island.

Later, Haití also agreed to do business with the islands of St. Thomas and Curacao. Contact with other countries was strictly limited, and Haitian ships were not allowed to travel to other islands in the Caribbean. As a result of this policy of isolation, Haitian trade with other countries quickly declined.

Haitian Control Brings Other Changes

The Boyer government brought many other changes to the island. The following were three important changes:

- All property belonging to the Spanish and French governments was taken over by the Haitian government. These properties included buildings, convents, land, horses, etc.

- The system of slavery was abolished on the eastern part of the island. Freedmen were given land and allowed to serve in the army.

- Citizens were not allowed to contact or do business with other governments. Citizens of other countries who lived on the island had to carry passports at all times.

President Boyer also tried to limit the power of the Roman Catholic Church, which owned a great deal of land in the former Spanish colony. Boyer nationalized this land by putting it under the control of his government. Later, he distributed this land to his followers and to freedmen. Boyer also tried to limit the power of the Church by removing priests and bishops from the government payroll.

The First Cathedral of Santo Domingo, built in 1514, was taken over, along with other church and colonial government property, by the Haitian government.

Boyer Seeks Support

In order to strengthen his government's control over the eastern part of Haití, Boyer wanted to bring people who were his supporters to that region. He had a plan to attract six thousand African Americans to the Republic of Haití, and proposed to grant them full civil and political rights. He sent Mr. J. Granville to the United States to encourage African Americans to come to Haití. Mr. Granville was successful. The first immigrants of African descent arrived in Santo Domingo in November 1824. Unfortunately, many of these immigrants died of typhus fever. Those who stayed in the cities of Santo Domingo and Samaná survived, and many of their descendants live there today.

Recognition By France

Boyer also hoped to strengthen his government by gaining recognition from France. In 1825, he sent a commission to France for this purpose. Almost a year later, the French king, Charles X, agreed to recognize Haití under certain conditions:

- France would recognize the western part of the island, but not the eastern part or former Spanish colony.
- Haití would pay 150 million francs to French colonists who had lost their land after independence.
- French ships would now be allowed to come into Haití and would pay only one-half of the duty or fee that ships from other countries paid.

Boyer agreed to the French king's terms. In order to raise money to pay former French colonists as the king requested, Boyer increased taxes to citizens on both parts of the island. Because of this taxation and because they did not want to be dominated again by the French, many Haitians resented the Boyer-France "Treaty of Recognition."

Although Boyer's government tried to bring about reforms, many problems remained. For example, Boyer was unable to make the promised payments to France even after raising taxes. As a penalty, the French government increased the interest payments on money that Haití had borrowed. This caused Haití to become deeper in debt. Other problems resulted from the government policy of isolation, which caused trade to decline. Because business slowed, many people could not get jobs. Poverty increased, and the economy of the country became weaker. Also, attempts to improve agriculture had not been successful. As a result of these problems, large numbers of people left Haití and resettled in Cuba, Puerto Rico, and Venezuela.

Separatist Movements in the Spanish Territory of Haití: 1833-1844

Many people in the eastern part of the island wanted to break away from Haitian rule. They wanted to be independent. There were at least five different groups who wanted to separate from Haití. These groups were called "separatists." Each had its own goals. The strongest

Manual de Historia Dominicana, Frank Moya Pons

JUAN PABLO DUARTE

group, called the Trinitaria Secret Society, was founded and led by Juan Pablo Duarte. Other well-known leaders of this group were Matías Ramón Mella and Francisco del Rosario Sánchez. The members of the Society pledged their property and lives to establish a country free from all foreign control. They wanted to call this country "La República Dominicana" (Dominican Republic). They referred to the inhabitants of the former Spanish Colony as Dominicans. The Trinitaria Society became popular because many citizens and soldiers were not satisfied with the Haitian government.

When his economic plans to develop Haití failed, Boyer resigned and left the country. The Haitian Senate then elected General Charles Herard as President of the Republic. In the meantime, the Trinitaria movement continued to gain strength. The city of Santo Domingo was the center of this movement. Interest in breaking away from Haití spread through many towns and cities. During the elections of 1843, most members elected to the town councils were in favor of separating from Haití. Dominicans for and against independence wrote pamphlets and made speeches. Anti-Haitian feeling increased, and strengthened the road to independence.

The Last Days of Haitian Control

President Charles Herard was aware of the increasing strength of the independence movement. In response, he tried to gain back the people's faith in the Haitian government by condemning some abuses that were committed by Haitian officials. He also freed some people who had been put in jail because they were against the Haitian government. However, Herard believed in the indivisibility of the Haitian Republic, and his aim was to crush the independence movement.

One Island "Indivisible"

Independence is Declared

In 1843, Dominicans learned that Herard was planning a tour of Santo Domingo. News spread that the President had ordered separatist leaders put in jail. Matías Ramón Mella and other leaders were sent to prison in Port-au-Prince.

Herard arrived in Santo Domingo on July 12, 1843. Only Haitians, Dominicans in favor of the Haitian government, and a few curious observers greeted the president. He ordered all prisoners released from Santo Domingo's jails. In exchange, he imprisoned fifteen men who were accused of plotting against the Haitian Republic. Herard hoped to imprison Trinitarian leaders, including Juan Pablo Duarte and Francisco del Rosario Sánchez, but they were able to escape.

The leaders of the Trinitarian movement who remained free continued to work for independence. They were able to persuade an important official of the Haitian government, Mr. Tomás Bobadilla, to join the independence movement. Bobadilla had many followers. His support added credit and power to the Trinitaria movement.

More and more Dominicans from other regions of the country began to agree that their country should be independent from Haití. Trinitaria leaders and their followers decided to declare Dominican independence. On the night of February 27, 1844, they met in the city of Santo Domingo at the Gate of La Misericordia. They fired a loud shot as a symbol of their independence. The next day, Francisco del Rosario Sánchez met with Haitian government officials to arrange the details of Haitian withdrawal from the Dominican Republic. The Haitians agreed to give up the Spanish territory because they realized that they were too weak to defeat the Dominicans, and because both sides wanted to avoid bloodshed. After the Haitian government withdrew from the eastern part of the island, the Dominican Republic became an independent nation.

Shot fired at the Gate of La Misericordia as a symbol of independence.

Gate of La Misericordia

CHAPTER 4 REVIEW

I. **Vocabulary for Review**

   A. First, put the following words in alphabetical order. Then, using the glossary at the end of the book and a dictionary, write a definition for each word:

   assassinate, impact, abolish, blockade, persuade, influence, recognition, isolation, resign, condemn, symbol

   B. Use each word in a sentence of your own. Be sure to provide good context clues for the vocabulary word.

II. **Lesson Review**

   1. What did Haitian leaders mean when they said that Haití was "indivisible?"
   2. What did President Boyer do to limit the power of the Roman Catholic Church in the former Spanish colony?
   3. Why did President Boyer send J. Granville to the United States?
   4. List three changes that came about after the Haitian invasion of the Spanish colony in 1822.
   5. a) What was the purpose of La Trinitaria Society?
      b) Name some of its leaders.
   6. What happened at the Gate of La Misericordia on February 27, 1844? What was the result of that night's events?

III. **Critical Thinking and Writing**

   It is 1818. President Jean Pierre Boyer of Haití believes the entire island should be one country, all of it controlled by Haití. You agree with Boyer. You know some government officials living in Santo Domingo, and President Boyer has asked you to write to one of these officials. In your letter, try to convince him to work for a united country.

IV. **Enrichment Exercise**

   In this chapter, you read that Dominicans had strong feelings for and against independence. They wrote speeches to try to get others to agree with their point of view. Pretend that you live in Santo Domingo. It is the year 1843. Write a speech in favor of or in opposition to Santo Domingo's independence from Haití. Present your speech to your class.

CHAPTER

5

The Experience of Independence

Gonzalo Briones/Listín Diario

After independence, Dominicans worked very hard to develop their new country. Within the Dominican Republic there were many groups, each group holding different ideas about how to run the country. Some Dominicans wanted complete independence without foreign control. Others wanted to be annexed to a European country. Still others wanted to be annexed to the United States. For many years, these groups struggled against each other for power over the new Republic.

The First Period of Dominican Self-Rule: 1844-1861

On the Day of Independence (February 27, 1844), Francisco del Rosario Sánchez called together a temporary government made up of seven members. This government was called a junta.[1] When Juan Pablo Duarte, the mastermind of Dominican independence, returned from exile, the junta asked him to be President and Chief Commander of the Republic. Because Duarte thought that the president should be elected, not appointed, he did not accept the offer. The junta then appointed Tomás Bobadilla president.

In the meantime, Haití was planning to seize control of the Dominican Republic. A month after the Republic gained independence, Haitian troops began their attack. President Bobadilla appointed Pedro Santana, General

Tomás Pastoriza

Juan Pablo Duarte

of the Dominican Liberation Army. Santana had supported the Trinitaria movement during the fight for independence. Now, his mission was to stop the Haitians. Four months later, Santana was able to defeat the invading Haitian troops.

Pedro Santana

The Rule of Santana

By defeating Haitian troops, Santana became a powerful military leader. When he returned to the city of Santo Domingo, he did away with the junta and set up his own government. Santana exiled Dominican patriots and independence leaders such as Duarte, Sánchez, and Mella.

---

[1] A junta is a small group of military leaders who take charge of a government, usually after the previous government has been overthrown.

Duarte was exiled to Germany. Others were exiled to Curacao, Puerto Rico, St. Thomas, and the United States. He killed other patriots such as María Trinidad Sánchez. Santana became president of the Republic and served until 1848. Later, he would serve three more terms.

María Trinidad Sánchez was a Dominican patriot. She wanted the Dominican Republic to be independent without any foreign control. Sánchez was against the dictatorship of Pedro Santana and was part of a group who tried to bring exiled Dominicans back to the Dominican Republic. She is also known for creating the first hand-made Dominican flag. María Trinidad Sánchez spoke out against the cruelty of Santana. As a result, he ordered her to be hung in 1845, on the first anniversary of the Dominican Independence.

During Santana's first term, he set up Electoral Assemblies in order to elect a Dominican Congress. The Congress then wrote a Constitution which decreed that the Dominican Republic was a "free nation, independent and sovereign." Along with these written principles of democracy, the Constitution gave Santana the power of a dictator. This allowed him to take control of the country. In order to maintain order and remove those who did not support him, he jailed, exiled, or killed his opponents. Tomás Bobadilla said, "Santana has become a tyrant." Following are some of the things that happened during Santana's first term:

- He took all property from land owners and from the previous government.
- He allowed only the Roman Catholic religion to be practiced.
- He appointed men who were loyal to him as governors of the five Dominican provinces.
- He organized the armed forces and set up a military draft.
- He tried to gain recognition from the United States and protection from Spain and France, but these plans failed.

Serious conflicts developed between Santana and many others in the country. His harsh dictatorship caused the National Congress to oppose him and he lost popular support because poverty had increased. In addition, Santana did not get along with Roman Catholic leaders. He also lost the support of the wealthy. Because his support was greatly weakened, Santana resigned as president.

Governments of Presidents Jiménez and Báez: 1848-1853

After Santana left the presidency, General Manuel Jiménez was elected the next president of the Republic. He served for a brief term of nine months. During this time, the Dominican Congress wrote a Decree of Amnesty for Dominicans who had been exiled by Santana for their political ideas. The amnesty, or pardon, allowed independence leaders to return to the country and enjoy political freedom.

Buenaventura Báez

In 1849, when the Haitians attacked the Dominican Republic again, Congress asked Santana to help the government. Santana assembled a large number of troops, and defeated the Haitians. Once again, victory increased Santana's power. He marched on the capital and declared himself dictator. Jiménez fled the country and went into exile. However, Santana was unwilling to be president of the country again. General Buenaventura Báez, who had the support of Congress, claimed the office and served his first term as president from 1849 to 1853. (He served four additional terms at other times.) During his first term, President Báez was able to keep the Haitians from invading the Dominican Republic. He also helped the country to become more stable.

Santana Returns for a Second Term

Because of the constant threat of Haitian invasion, the government needed a strong military leader. This situation made it possible for Pedro Santana to return to the presidency in 1853. During his second term, Santana declared himself above the Constitution. This meant that, when he chose, he did not have to follow the Constitution. He exiled Báez from the country, and blamed many Dominican problems on him. He mistreated the clergy who had supported Báez, and exiled respected church leaders and educators. Many people resented Santana's rule, and conflict soon developed between those who supported him and those who supported Báez. Santana resigned once again, and Báez returned to power in 1856.

Báez Returns for a Second Term

Báez returned to power from 1856 to 1858. During his second term as president, Báez signed a peace treaty with Haití. However, his plans to improve the economy brought serious troubles. His attempt to control the country's tobacco business upset the growers of the Cibao region, who wanted to control their own affairs. Merchants, property owners, and concerned citizens of the Cibao region protested Báez's economic policies. In 1857, these citizens declared a separate government in the city of Santiago.

Santana Returns for a Third Term

The leader of the Santiago government, Desiderio Valverde, organized an armed revolution to overthrow Báez. In 1858, Valverde and the Cibao government wrote a constitution which promised political and civil rights and abolished capital punishment.

At this time, Pedro Santana was living in exile. Valverde and the Cibao government decided to bring Santana back to join the revolt against Báez. Santana came back under the condition that the country would return to the Constitution of 1854. This meant that Santana would have complete control again. Santana's supporters were more powerful than the Cibao government and the Báez government, and began to take control of the country.

Santana sent his troops to cities in the north to convince the members of the Cibao revolt to join his forces. Santana himself marched with troops to the city of Santiago, where Cibao leaders agreed to join him. The Santiago government agreed to Santana's proposal, and its leaders left the country as soon as they had a chance. President Báez also went into exile.

On June 13, 1858, Pedro Santana was re-elected president for the third time. During this term, there was a serious economic crisis. Paper money printed by the prior governments had no value and the government became bankrupt. Disease and starvation hit the country. Although Santana had more money printed, the people had no faith in its value. The government had to borrow money from local businesses in order to operate. Meanwhile, Santana had secretly made plans to annex the Dominican Republic to Spain.

Spanish Rule: 1861-1865

The annexation of the Dominican Republic to Spain occurred in March 1861, ending seventeen years of Dominican self-rule. The country was once again ruled by Spain. Spanish troops sent from Puerto Rico and Cuba enforced harsh laws on the Dominican people. Dominicans were forced to pay heavy taxes, and non-Catholics were persecuted. President Santana, who had delivered the Republic to Spain, was given a royal rank in Spain's army and a lifetime pension of twelve thousand pesos.

Over the next four years, there were repeated conflicts between the Spanish forces and Dominicans who wanted the Spaniards to leave the country. Dominican patriots living in Haití organized a guerrilla movement to overthrow Spanish rule.[2] Fighting broke out in Santiago and other places. The military government of Spain responded by throwing many innocent people into prison. During these conflicts, thousands of Dominicans and Spaniards were wounded or killed.

During the period of Spanish rule (1861-1865), Dominican patriots were thrown into the jail or killed by Spanish forces.

Almost six thousand Spanish soldiers died of yellow fever during this time. By July 1865, Spain had given up the fight. Spanish troops left the Dominican Republic, and a second Dominican Independence was declared.

The Second Period of Dominican Self-Rule: 1865-1916

The four-year fight to remove Spain from the Dominican Republic caused great turmoil. By the time that independence was declared, the country was in a major crisis. Dominicans were divided, and different groups struggled for control. Two major political parties developed: the Blue and the Red. Blue Party members wanted the Dominican people to have a stronger role in government and more economic opportunities. The Red Party favored strong government control and few civil rights.

---

[2] A guerrilla movement is developed by a group of volunteer fighters who are trying to overthrow the government. At first, a guerrilla movement is organized in secret. Usually, people in the movement try to gain control over a region of the countryside. From that base, they attack the forces of the government in power.

United States President Ulysses S. Grant sent a commission of five men to the Dominican Republic to study the possibility of its annexation to the United States. One of the commissioners was Frederick Douglass (far left above), internationally known abolitionist leader.

Báez Returns

In 1868, Buenaventura Báez was able to return to power as leader of the Red party. During this period of Dominican history, the United States was fighting its own civil war. After the war was over, President Báez tried to convince the United States to annex the Dominican Republic. United States President Ulysses S. Grant was in favor of annexation. He tried to convince members of Congress to support this idea. However, Senator Charles Sumner, along with many other U.S. Congressmen were against annexation. Sumner believed that the Dominican Republic should remain independent. Because of his belief, many Dominicans think of Senator Sumner as a great U.S. leader.

Luperón Overthrows Báez and Brings Change

Conflicts continued between the Red and Blue Parties. In 1878, General Gregorio Luperón, the leader of the Blue Party, succeeded in overthrowing Báez and his Red Party. Luperón set up a temporary government in Puerto Plata. During his two years as president, he helped exiled patriots from other countries in the Caribbean. He gave support to Eugenio María de Hostos and Ramón Emeterio Betances of Puerto Rico, and to Antonio Maceo of Cuba. Eugenio María de Hostos lived in Santo Domingo for nine years (1879-1888). He founded a system of secondary schools and teachers' colleges. He is known for greatly improving the standard of education in the Dominican Republic. (See p. 83.)

Manual de Historia Dominicana, Frank Moya Pons

GENERAL GREGORIO LUPERON

Stability Leads to Modernization

In 1880, Fernando Arturo de Meriño was elected president. Like Lupeón, he was a member of the Blue Party. Meriño granted pardons to Dominicans who had been accused of crimes against the government. He also supported free press, improvements in education, and the publication of literature, scientific works, and independent newspapers. For the first time under Dominican self-rule, there was a stable period. Elections were called for the next president, and the government passed smoothly from Meriño to General Ulises Heureaux, who was elected president in 1882. The Dominican people gave him the nickname "Lilís" (Lee-lee).

Lilís' first term of office was from 1882 to 1884. During this time, he worked to improve public schools and health education, and to establish a military hospital. After three years out of office, he began his second term in 1887. During this term, the first newspaper was published in the Dominican Republic. It was called El Listín Diario. This newspaper helped to inform Dominicans about daily events.

General Ulises Heureaux

After this, Lilís served four terms in a row. From 1887 until 1889, he was successful in bringing Dominicans together and was well liked by many people. He helped others to develop a sense of pride in being Dominican. Lilís was a practical man who was determined to bring order to government, and to build more respect for the law. He also granted pardons to those who were exiled or in prison for political reasons. He gave many of these people jobs in his government.

*In 1989, **El Listín Diario** was 100 years old.*
Today, it is one of the major newspapers in the Dominican Republic.

President Lilís wanted to modernize the Dominican Republic. He wanted to bring Dominicans out of their poverty. In order to do so, he arranged for loans from other countries and used the money to build roads and schools. Lilís improved agriculture, developed a railroad system, and introduced the telegraph. He also opened up trade relations for his country with the United States.

Independent Picture Service

Lilís improved agriculture in the Dominican Republic and developed a railroad system. He also introduced the telegraph and opened up trade with the United States.

Dictatorship Develops

Many of the changes brought by Lilís were for the good of the country. However, Lilís had developed a very powerful government in order to carry out his plans. Whenever he learned about a plot against him or his government, he had the leaders killed. In short, Lilís had become a dictator. Although he was a member of the Blue Party, he did not put the Party's ideas into practice. Many Dominicans turned against him. In 1899, Lilís was shot and killed while on a tour of the country.

The next seventeen years of Dominican self-rule were years of turmoil. There were many leaders, but most seemed more interested in personal gain than in the good of the country. A total of thirteen presidents and five juntas led the Dominican Republic between 1899 and 1916. That year, an invasion by the United States ended the Dominican Republic's second period of self-rule.

CHAPTER 5 REVIEW

I. Vocabulary for Review

A. First, put the following words in alphabetical order. Then, using the glossary at the end of the book and a dictionary, write definitions for the following words:

> annex, exile, decreed, opponents, dictatorial, tyrant, sovereign, resign, persecute, turmoil

B. Use each word in a sentence of your own. Be sure to provide good context clues for the vocabulary word.

II. Lesson Review

1. Who masterminded the successful independence movement of 1844?

2. Why didn't Pablo Duarte become President and Chief Commander of the new Republic?

3. Why did Santana resign from the presidency in 1848?

4. During his third term as president, Santana made a secret plan with Spain. What was the result of this plan?

5. What disease killed many Spanish soldiers in the Dominican Republic between 1861 and 1865?

6. What nickname was given to General Ulises Heureaux? What were some of his achievements?

7. What invasion ended the second period of the Dominican Republic's self-rule?

III. Critical Writing and Thinking

A. Lilís served five terms as president of the Dominican Republic. He was a member of the Blue Party, but he sometimes acted against the Blue Party's beliefs. He helped to develop the country, but he also became a dictator. If you had been living at that time, would you have been one of his followers? Explain why or why not in a paragraph.

B. Make two lists which compare the first and second periods of Dominican self-rule.

CHAPTER

Politics of the Modern Period

Maximo Pou

Tony Frank

Honorable Presidente Joaquin Balaguer

Printed with permission from the **Dominican Republic: A Caribbean Crucible**; by H.J. Wiarda and M.J. Kryzanek, Westview Press, Inc. © 1982.

During the seventeen years following the death of President Lilís (1899), there was great turmoil in the Dominican Republic. As different groups fought for power, the economy of the country was neglected. Government loans from other countries were not repaid, and the country became bankrupt. European nations began to demand payment of their loans. Several of these countries sent gunboats to the Dominican Republic, hoping to force the Dominican government to pay back the money. These actions led to an invasion of the Dominican Republic by the United States in 1916. Beginning in 1930, after the departure of United States troops, the harsh dictatorship of Rafael Trujillo brought some improvements to the country, but Dominicans lost most of their civil, political, and human rights. Gaining economic and political stability has been the challenge of the modern period in the Dominican Republic.

United States Involvement

In the first part of the 1900's, the United States was a major world power. The Caribbean was an important area to the United States, because many American businesses had invested money in countries like Puerto Rico and Cuba. In addition, the Panama Canal provided a short cut for ships traveling between the Atlantic and Pacific Oceans beginning in 1914. For example, a ship carrying goods from San Francisco no longer had to go all the way around South America to get to New York City. (See map on this page.) This arrangement saved time and money. The United States also considered the Panama Canal and islands in the Caribbean important to its military protection. The Canal could be used to carry supplies in case of a war. Certain Caribbean islands could be used as fueling stops for ships, as well as sites for army and navy bases.

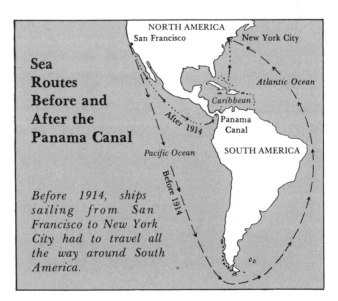

Sea Routes Before and After the Panama Canal

NORTH AMERICA
San Francisco
New York City
Atlantic Ocean
Caribbean
After 1914
Panama Canal
Pacific Ocean
SOUTH AMERICA
Before 1914

Before 1914, ships sailing from San Francisco to New York City had to travel all the way around South America.

Use of the Monroe Doctrine

In the early 1900's, the United States applied the Monroe Doctrine to keep other nations out of the Caribbean and the rest of Latin America. The ideas of this doctrine were stated by President James Monroe in 1823, when he said that the United States would not allow Europeans to interfere in the affairs of any country in the Americas. If they did, the action would be viewed as a threat to the safety of the United States. In this way, the United States attempted to decrease the power of European countries in the affairs of the Dominican Republic and other Latin American countries.

The "Big Stick"

In 1904, President Theodore Roosevelt issued the Roosevelt Corollary to the Monroe Doctrine. This statement said that the United States had the right to take action if Latin American nations did not pay their debts. The United States thus took upon itself the authority to police the Americas. In issuing his Corollary, Roosevelt said: "Speak softly and carry a big stick, and you will go far." Roosevelt used this policy, called the "big stick" policy, in dealing with several Latin American countries.

United States Takes Action

When European countries sent their gunboats to the Dominican Republic to collect money owed to them, U.S. President Theodore Roosevelt and Dominican President Ramón Cáceres developed the Agreement of 1907.

This agreement gave the United States power to take over the collection of custom duties paid on goods coming into the

Tomás Pastoriza

Ramón Cáceres served as president from 1905 to 1911.

Dominican Republic. More than half of the money raised from custom duties was used to pay Dominican foreign debts. Because so much money was sent out of the country, there was less money to spend on education, housing, health care, farming and industry. Even so, Cáceres was able to bring about

History and Museums Division, U.S. Marine Corps

U.S. Marines are on the warf at Monte Cristo. The building marked ADUANA is the customs house which was controlled by the United States during Cáceres' term as president.

some improvements in the Dominican Republic. During his term of office, roads, railroads, and the telegraph system were improved. Cáceres also tried to reform and upgrade the military, while he kept it under his control.

In 1911, Cáceres was assassinated by an old rival. Several presidents followed him in a short period of time. Different groups

Painting of the assassination of President Cáceres by Rodríguez Urdaneta.

fought each other for power, and there were many revolts in the country.

Even though some Dominican groups were against it, the United States wanted to stay involved in Dominican affairs. By 1912, the United States had taken control of the Dominican treasury. The United States also tried to limit European involvement in the Dominican Republic. For example, Germany had been buying tobacco from the island. The United States was at war with Germany at this time (World War I), and did not want Germany to have dealings with the Dominican Republic. In addition, the United States used the Dominican Republic as a market for its goods, and as a source of low-cost natural resources, food products, and laborers. Huge profits could be made by American companies who set up businesses in the Dominican Republic.

United States Military Rule

By 1916, fighting and revolts around the country made it difficult for Americans to do business with the Dominican Republic. The United States wanted to stop these revolts, and sent Marines to invade the island on November 26, 1916. The Dominican Republic was placed under United States military rule. Following were some of the results:

U.S. Marines camped outside Santo Domingo six months after the United States invaded the Dominican Republic.

- The United States took control of the Dominican economy. This meant that the United States was in charge of all exports and imports.

- American corporations dominated the sugar industry. In 1925, the value of exported sugar was almost sixty three million dollars.

- All imports to the Dominican Republic (such as cars, agricultural equipment, cotton, hats, silk, paper, steel, paint, soap, glass, liquor, cosmetics, and chemical products) came from the United States.

- Roads, railroads, communication, and health care were improved.

- National guerrilla movements were for the most part destroyed.

- A National Guard was set up.

- The United States Haina Military Academy was set up to train Dominican officers. Within a few years, this training created a military elite in the country.

- Politics were controlled by a small group of landowners and military leaders under the influence of the United States. The Dominican people had very little say in running their own government. There were no elections. Thus, the possibility of democracy during these years of occupation was decreased.

The End of United States Military Rule

There were many citizens in both countries who were against United States military rule of the Dominican Republic. In the 1920 United States presidential election, the Republican candidate, Warren G. Harding, took a stand against United States control of the Dominican Republic. Other Latin American nations also opposed American control of the Dominican Republic.

In 1921, the American press demanded an investigation of abuses that United States Marines were accused of committing against the Dominican people. The United States Senate investigated these charges, and received testimony from Dominican citizens to support the accusations. Protest against American control of the Dominican Republic increased, and led to a withdrawal of troops in 1924.

In the early 1890's, Señorita Ercilia Pepín was a teacher of math and science who trained students to be teachers. She also defended equal rights for women and spoke out against the military occupation of the United States (1916-1924). Today, a park, street and two schools are named after Señorita Pepín.

Many Dominicans were against United States military rule of their country. Some were armed and ready to fight. In the picture below, United States Marines search for weapons in Dominican homes.

Rafael L. Trujillo's Regime: 1930-1961

Six years after the United States removed its troops from the Dominican Republic, Rafael Trujillo was elected its president. Trujillo was a graduate of the United States Haina Military Academy. He moved up quickly in his military career, promoted first to lieutenant colonel and then to chief of the National Police. When Trujillo wanted to be president, he used the power of the army to threaten those who did not support him. He even threw his opponent, Federico Velázquez, into jail. By the time of the election, anyone who spoke out against Trujillo had to leave the country or face death.

First inauguration of Trujillo (center) as president in 1930.

Trujillo built monuments and public works projects. Many, such as the statue above, were built in his honor. In 1960, after his assassination, the citizens of Santo Domingo destroyed this statue which was located at the National University of Santo Domingo.

Improvements, But At What Price?

During his first term as president, Trujillo set up a one party system to increase his power. He began by building monuments and public works projects in the city of Santo Domingo. He promoted agriculture and health care. Within ten years, Trujillo

Evangelina Rodríguez was the first Dominican woman to become a doctor in the Dominican Republic. Although it was too dangerous to oppose Trujillo openly, she was not in support of him. Rodríguez spent her life serving poor people in her country.

was able to pay the foreign debt owed to the United States, and was given the title of "Restorer of the Dominican Financial Sovereignty." [1]

Trujillo also promoted education. However, he used the schools to increase his power. He had history textbooks written which described him as the greatest defender of the Dominican Republic.

Before Trujillo, the government of the Dominican Republic changed hands many times. Leaders did not remain in power long. However, Trujillo was able to remain in office for thirty one years. Under his regime, Dominicans lost their civil, political, and human rights. Trujillo terrorized the country with a secret

---

[1] "Sovereignty" means complete independence, a country's control over its own government.

service squad. His opponents were tortured, imprisoned, or killed. He accused any person or group against him of being a communist, and used anti-communist propaganda to remove his opponents.

One of the major crimes of the Trujillo government was the massacre of more than twenty thousand Haitians living in the Dominican Republic. Trujillo tried to make Dominicans believe that Haitian people were a threat to the country. Today, many historians believe that Trujillo's attack against Haitians (who are largely a Black people) was based on racism. It is known that Trujillo favored the Spanish culture and tried to limit aspects of African culture in the Dominican Republic.

María Teresa Mirabal

Minerva Mirabal

Patria Mirabal

The three Mirabal sisters openly protested against the lack of freedom of speech under Trujillo's rule. They were captured and tortured to death by government officials in 1960.

In the Dominican Republic, only Trujillo ruled. Trujillo ignored the Constitution, and made decisions based on his own will. He controlled the legal system through force, built a dictatorship based on fear, and used his personality to increase his power. For example, he organized marches and demonstrations in his own honor. He also changed the name of the city of Santo Domingo to Ciudad Trujillo (City of Trujillo).

Support for Trujillo

The United States supported the Trujillo regime. Some of this support came from the United States' policy toward Latin America. In 1933, President Franklin D. Roosevelt, who wanted to change United States relations with Latin America, developed an approach called the "good neighbor" policy. According to this policy, the United States would try not to interfere in the affairs of other countries in the Americas. The policy was used as a reason not to oppose Trujillo.

Another reason given for support of Trujillo was his anti-communist stand. Beginning in 1945, the United States and the Soviet Union had many disagreements. Tension grew between the two nations and came to be known as the "cold war." Each country wanted to have the most influence on the other countries of the world. Because of its rivalry with the Soviet Union, the United States was in favor of Latin American leaders, such as Trujillo, who were anti-communist. The United States' attack on communism in Latin American countries grew stronger in the 1960's. By this time, the United States had developed a strong anti-Soviet policy in Latin America. Even with these reasons, many people thought that the United States was wrong to support a dictator who denied civil and human rights to the masses of people in the Dominican Republic.

The End of the Trujillo Regime

The rule of Trujillo lasted until May 1961. At that time, he was killed by a small group of military officers. Trujillo's family tried to take control after his death, but they were forced to leave the country. Vice President Joaquín Balaguer became the next president. His government lasted only a short time, due to the unrest caused by thirty years of Trujillo's repression, and by the people's reaction against lack of civil and political rights.[2]

Trujillo was assassinated in 1961.

Vice President Joaquín Balaguer became president after Trujillo's assassination.

---

[2] Repression is strict and severe control. It prevents natural expression and development.

Current History

The first free and democratic election in forty years was held in the Dominican Republic in 1962. Professor Juan Bosch, who had been in exile since the early 1930's, was elected president. He was a candidate of the Dominican Revolutionary Party (PRD), which he had begun while in exile. The PRD Party had a large popular following because it promised democracy and many social reforms. The Roman Catholic Church, the military, and old ruling groups were against these changes because they feared that they would lose

Former President Juan Bosch

power. They accused Bosch of being a communist because he was willing to allow all political groups to exist in the Dominican Republic. In 1963, there was a military coup which ended Bosch's government after only seven months.[3] With such a short term, his program for economic and social justice made little progress.

After Bosch returned to exile, the military took control of the government. Several groups with different interests tried to gain enough strength to come to power. Conflicts between these groups became serious, and the PRD moved to seize power by taking over the Presidential Palace. PRD members and some members of the military wanted to bring Juan Bosch back to lead the country.

The United States Sends Troops

United States leaders did not want Juan Bosch and the PRD to return to power in the Dominican Republic. They thought that, if Bosch were president, the Dominican Republic would lean toward communism. They tried to stop the revolution led by the PRD by sending twenty three thousand troops to invade the Dominican Republic. United States President Lyndon Johnson said that he sent troops to protect United States citizens and defend the interests of American businesses in the Dominican Republic. These troops fought against the revolutionary forces, and defeated them within six months.

---

[3] A military coup (from the French term "coup d'état") is the overthrow of a government by force.

Dominican women, yelling "Go Home Yankees" to U.S. Marines, protest the military intervention of 1965.

The presence of United States troops in the Dominican Republic caused strong anti-American feelings. Many people felt that the Revolution of 1965 was an attempt by Dominicans to control their own destiny. They believed that this attempt was crushed by the interference of the United States.

Balaguer Elected President

Even though Juan Bosch was allowed to return from exile and run for president in 1966, he and his followers faced constant threats and attacks from the police and

Master Dominican artist Yoryi Morel depicted poverty in rural areas in the painting shown above, entitled "Campesino cibaeño."

military forces. The United States supported Dr. Joaquín Balaguer, who was able to move easily around the country and campaign. Dr. Balaguer won the 1966 presidential election, and was elected again in 1970 and 1974. He served until 1978. With support from the United States, he was able to bring some changes to the Dominican Republic. He built schools, housing projects, dams, bridges, and clinics. Even so, unemployment was high and the largest part of the population still lived in poverty.

Most of the country's new resources stayed in the hands of the wealthy or the middle class. The middle class, which made up about 15% of the population, included government workers, army officers, small business owners, students, teachers, doctors, lawyers, and union leaders. The middle class grew with the progress of the Balaguer government.

Even though the middle class has been growing, the poor continue to make up about 80% of the people in the Dominican Republic. On the left is a home of an upper middle class family. On the right is a home of a poor family.

In 1978, Balaguer was defeated by **PRD** candidate Silvestre Antonio Guzmán. Guzmán allowed greater political freedom and supported human rights, such as freedom of speech. People were allowed to express their views about government without as much fear of punishment. Guzmán put money into building new schools and into programs for people in poverty. In 1982, Guzmán died suddenly. It was said that he committed suicide, although some people thought that he may have been murdered.

President Antonio Guzmán in 1979.

Printed with permission from the Dominican Republic: A Caribbean Crucible: by H.J. Wiarda and M.J. Kryzanek, Westview Press, Inc. © 1982.

During the early 1980's, there was a great deal of political and social tension because of the country's economy. Prices of goods were very high. There was public unrest, and there were demonstrations and clashes between the police and political groups. Many people were arrested, and many others died as a result of clashes with the police during 1984 and 1985.

Balaguer Returns

Elections were held in May 1986, and Balaguer won by a small number of votes. He had promised to reduce poverty in the country, and to allow different points of view about government. People hoped that this would bring about better cooperation among political parties.

Dr. Balaguer is currently the president of the Dominican Republic (1989). He has played a role in Dominican politics for many years. Balaguer served under Trujillo, yet he acts very differently from Trujillo. He holds many conservative ideas.[4] His style of leadership is paternalistic. This means that he is a father figure in Dominican politics. Balaguer writes about Dominican history, and is also a fine orator.

In recent years, the Dominican government has tried to develop tourism (above left) and manufacturing for foreign markets (above right) in order to decrease the country's dependence on the production and sale of sugar.

[4] Conservative ideas often favor keeping things the way they are, and usually avoid change.

CHAPTER 6 REVIEW

I. Vocabulary for Review
A. First, put the following words in alphabetical order. Then, using the glossary at the end of the book and a dictionary, write definitions for the following words:

> bankrupt, turmoil, doctrine, testimony, propaganda, terrorized, regime, interfere, elite, communism, racism

B. Use each word in a sentence of your own. Be sure to provide good context clues for the vocabulary word.

II. Lesson Review
1. Why did the Caribbean islands become so important to the United States in the first part of the 1900's?
2. How did the United States use the Monroe Doctrine and the Roosevelt Corollary to keep European countries out of the Dominican Republic?
3. List two ways in which American businesses benefited as a result of United States military control of the Dominican Republic between 1916 and 1924.
4. During the Trujillo regime, some people said that, "the Constitution is not worth the paper it was written on." List two reasons why this may have been said.
5. Why did the United States support Dr. Joaquín Balaguer, and not Juan Bosch?

III. Critical Thinking and Writing
A. Write a short story about the Trujillo regime. You may use fictional characters in your story, but be sure to use information from this text and other sources in order to create an accurate historical context.
B. Use your school or local library to write a biography on Dr. Joaquín Balaguer. You may include information on his personal, political, literary, and oratorical activities.

IV. Enrichment Exercise
Your name is Warren G. Harding. It is 1920 and you are running for the office of president of the United States. Write a campaign speech in which you take a stand against United States control of the Dominican Republic. Try to find actual speeches or writings of Harding that discuss the relationship of the United States to the Dominican Republic.

CHAPTER

Dominican Society:
Past and Present

Culture is the total way of life of a society. The ideas, values, and what people produce over centuries make up culture. The language, art, literature, religion, economy, technology, politics, customs, and social organization of each society are all part of its culture.

In Chapter 1, you read about the culture of the early inhabitants of the Dominican Republic. At that time, the Dominican Republic was called Quisqueya or Haití. The culture of Quisqueya changed with the arrival of Spanish and African peoples. The blending of these cultures during the colonial period laid the foundation for the Dominican Republic today. Even though the social structure is divided into classes, Dominicans share many common traditions.

The Early Foundation

Before the invasion of the Spaniards, the Taíno had developed a way of life to suit their environment. Most were farmers or skilled craftsmen. Their way of life was communal. This means that they depended on each other, and lived and worked closely together. They often traveled to and traded with neighboring islands. All this changed when the Spaniards arrived and attempted to control the island and the people. The Taíno resisted these attempts, and fought the Spaniards. Thousands of Taíno died in these wars, as well as from the cruel abuse of and the diseases brought by the Spaniards. By the mid-1500's, very few of the original inhabitants were alive.

The city of Santo Domingo was the earliest site of Spanish colonial culture in the Americas. Early Spanish colonizers came from the kingdom of Castile in Spain. Some of these colonizers were landowners and cattle ranchers. Others were bishops, priests, soldiers, and public servants. The colonists brought their customs, language, legal system, economy, religion, and architecture with them. They also brought products like sugar cane, and guns, and introduced animals like dogs, cattle, and chickens. Today, Dominicans of Spanish ancestry are seen in all classes. However, the long-lasting effect of their colonial power causes them to be seen more often among the middle class and the wealthy.

Some scientists believe that African people came to the Americas even before Columbus. (See pp. 19-23). During the colonial period, large numbers of African people were brought to Quisqueya and forced to work in a system of slavery. They had skills in agriculture and other trades needed to develop the colonial economy. Many were metal workers, tailors, masons, ship builders, woodworkers, weavers and sculptors. Because of the harsh and long-lasting effects of slavery, Dominicans of African origin are mostly found among the poorest class in the Dominican Republic today. However, some are members of the middle class and upper class.

This campesino (farmer) owns no land. In order to feed his family, he works for other landowners.

This man owns a "colmado" (small store). It has everyday food needs such as beans, rice, salt, sugar, and canned goods. Other small stores carry fish or meat or frozen foods.

Polo is a sport played only by wealthy Dominicans.

Dominican mother and daughter.

Dominican Society Today

Dominican society today is based largely upon the Spanish colonial system of order, discipline, respect for authority, and power located at the head of the government. The president is the center of the system. He shapes the tone of the government and life in general through his "personalismo" (individual strengths and character).

The Roman Catholic Church is no longer as powerful in Dominican society as it used to be. Until recently, Church leaders represented one of the three most powerful groups in the country, along with the army and a small group of landowning families. Today, the Church has some influence on politics, and still plays a strong role in educational and in social and family matters.

In the Dominican Republic, church architecture reflects styles that range from early colonial to modern.

The small but powerful group of landowning families (often called the elite) is influential in industry today. Although landowners represent approximately 5% of the population, they have great influence in Dominican life because they have many financial resources, and the national economy depends on their industries to create jobs.

There is a growing urban middle class, representing 15% to 20% of the population. This group of small business owners, doctors, lawyers, teachers, students, union leaders, and government workers is generally in favor of an open society with less control by a few powerful families.

Today, approximately 6.4 million people live in the Dominican Republic. The seat of government is the capital city of Santo Domingo, which has a population of 1.3 million people.

Landowning families often operate plantations, such as the banana plantation above.

Since the 1950's, thousands of Dominicans have immigrated to the United States, living for the most part in New York City and other cities in the northeast. Other Dominicans live in Miami and in Puerto Rico. (See pp. 86-89.)

Approximately 80% of the population is very poor. Many are unemployed, or work at low paying jobs. Illiteracy, poor housing, malnutrition, and lack of basic services are part of daily life for this largest group of urban and rural Dominicans.

The three social groups, or classes —the wealthy, the middle class and the poor— are divided. Discrimination in the Dominican Republic is based largely on these class divisions. There is also discrimination against Haitians who cut sugar cane as immigrant workers. Some of the hostility toward Haitians is a reaction to the twenty-two years of Haitian rule (1822-1844). During his regime from 1930 to 1961, Rafael Trujillo actively promoted discrimination toward Haitians. (See p. 61.)

Common Traditions

Although there are three clearly divided classes, the people of each Dominican province share elements of heritage such as religious traditions. Each province has a patron saint, as well as colorful chants and popular dances. People devote time, money, and effort to preparing for the main religious festival of their town, city, or village. Each festival lasts for a week or more. The dances, music, and chants used in these festivals have been passed down from generation to generation, and many are a mixture of Taíno, Spanish, and African traditions. Although 90% of Dominicans are Roman Catholic, there are also small Protestant, Baptist, Bahai, Episcopalian, Evangelical, and Jewish congregations. Freedom of worship is protected by law in the Dominican Republic.

Dominicans have a reputation for being friendly, polite, and hospitable. Humor is an important part of their culture. Dominicans like jokes, and enjoy social and political satire on television and radio. Music, dancing, and sports are also enjoyed by most Dominicans. Although all types of sports are played, baseball is the most popular game among both children and adults. Dominicans play professional baseball in the Dominican Republic and in the United States. (See pp. 88-89.) The city of San Pedro de Macorís has produced many ball players for United States major league teams. Another popular sport is cock fighting. In this sport, roosters, usually wearing spurs, fight to the death.

Another activity that Dominicans enjoy is the "pasadía" (picnic). At the pasadías, Dominicans go to the beach and enjoy "arroz con pollo" (rice with chicken), roasted pig, and boiled or roasted plaintain. One popular national dish is called

Pasadía (picnic) at the beach.

"arroz, habichuelas y carnes" (rice, beans, and meats). Dominicans have nicknamed this dish "la bandera" (the flag) because it is so much a part of national tradition. People also enjoy natural fruit juices, rum, and beer.

The siesta (time for a nap after lunch) is also part of national custom and tradition. All work stops at noon, and begins again at 2:00 p.m. During siesta, most people go home, have lunch, and spend time with their families.

Dominicans celebrate many national holidays. Independence Day, celebrated on February 27th, is the country's most colorful celebration. To the right is a list of important holidays.

January 1	New Year's Day
January 6	Día de los Reyes (Epiphany)
January 16	Juan Pablo Duarte (Founding Father)
January 21	Our Lady of La Altagracia
February 27	Independence Day
Friday before Easter Sunday	Good Friday
April 14	Pan-American Day
May 1	Labor Day
July 16	Sociedad La Trinitaria Day
August 16	Restoration Day
September 24	Our Lady of Mercedes
October 12	Columbus Day
October 24	United Nations Day
November 1	All Saints Day
December 25	Christmas Day

The merengue is the most popular dance in the country. Young and old dance the merengue. There is a well-known saying, "El merengue revive a los muertos," which means, "The merengue will revive the dead." People move their bodies, tap their feet, and nod their heads to the rhythm of this lively dance. Instruments traditionally used for playing the merengue are the tambora, güiro, and acordeón. Often, the musicians also sing the merengue tunes. Today, merengue bands use woodwinds, brass, and drums. These modern instruments give more sound and color to merengue tunes. The words are very important, and deal with a variety of themes such as romance, tragedy, folklore, nature, patriotism, political protests, and current events. The bolero or slow tune is another popular type of music in the Dominican Republic.

Young and old dance the merengue.

El Nuevo Diario

73

Land and Resources

The Dominican Republic is 18,816 square miles in size, or two-thirds of the second largest island in the Caribbean. Haití occupies the other 1/3 of the island. The Dominican Republic has a variety of land forms, including mountains, rolling hills, valleys, lakes, rivers, and beaches.

The Cordillera Central is a large mountain range which runs east and west across the country and continues into Haití. This mountain range dips under the water (Caribbean Sea) on the east and west side of the island, and surfaces in Puerto Rico to the east and in Cuba to the west. The Cibao valley is north of the Cordillera. The fertile farmlands in the Cibao produce foods such as maize, beans, plantains, and rice. Dairy cattle are also raised and fed in the pastures of this fertile valley. The country has more than ten seaports which receive ocean going vessels, and there are a few rivers and lakes. Lago Enriquillo (named after Cacique Enriquillo, see p. 26) is the largest inland body of water in the Caribbean. It is thirty miles long and ten miles wide.

The climate of the Dominican Republic is mild year round. The westerly trade winds sweep over the island, and help to keep the atmosphere fresh and free of pollution. The climate supports the growth of various forms of plant life. Coconut palms, fruit-bearing trees, and plants such as orchids can be found in various regions of the country.

Fertile farmlands, forests of pines and hardwoods, fish, and minerals are important Dominican resources. Mahogany and satinwood are highly valued for making furniture. Lignum Vitae, a very hard wood, is used in shipbuilding. Other natural resources are fish such as kingfish, mackerel, red snapper, and shrimp, and underground metals such as gold, silver, and nickel. These minerals, which are exported from the country, bring in millions of dollars annually. The Dominican Republic also has the world's most important source of amber. This "gem" is actually fossilized pine resin that is twenty million years old.

The western hemisphere's largest known gold mine is in the Dominican Republic.

ARTS IN THE DOMINICAN REPUBLIC

There are many men and women in the Dominican Republic who are artists. Some are painters, and others are sculptors. Some make objects such as pottery for daily use. Dominican artists express a variety of themes. Some paint pictures of people and of nature, while others create paintings that depict historical or social issues. Sculptors often make public monuments, which can be seen in several Dominican cities.

Fernando Peña Defilló

Dominican sculptor (anonymous)

"Triumph of Love," 1972 by Peña Defilló.

Ada Balcácer stands in front of her painting.

A traditional potter finishes a large clay pot used for the storage of water. Pots like this one are used in areas where there is no running water.

Sculpture by Mario Cruz.

A carved wooden dujo (seat) of the Taíno.

Museum of Modern Art in La Plaza de la Cultura.

The "Palace of Fine Arts" has works of Dominican artists, as well as works of artists from around the world.

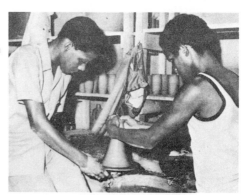

These young potters are studying at the National Center for Artisans in Santo Domingo.

DOMINICAN LITERATURE

Several examples of Spanish writing can be traced to the colony of Hispaniola. Friar Ramón Pané was commissioned by Christopher Columbus to study the religion of the original inhabitants of Hispaniola. His writing is thought to be the earliest known and written study of religion done in the Americas. Another famous piece of colonial literature is the *History of the Indies* by Father Bartolomé de las Casas. This work describes the colonial history of the Caribbean, including the harsh impact of colonization on the original inhabitants. Father Las Casas defended the rights of the Taíno, and used his writing to convince others that the colonizers' treatment of the Taíno was wrong.

Many Dominicans followed in the footsteps of these early Spanish writers. From the colonial period to the present, they have often written about social and political issues. For example, during Haitian rule of the island (1822-1844), many writers expressed their feelings about independence. After independence, Félix María del Monte created a short poetry form to describe social events. His writing was very patriotic, and he became known as the "Father of Dominican Literature." Many exiled patriots were also writers who expressed their sad and often bitter feelings about being forced to leave their country.

During the late 1800's and early 1900's, there were three major literary movements:

- Indigenismo (In-de-hay-NEES-mo): works about the culture and life of the original inhabitants.
- Criollismo (Cre-ol-LYEES-mo): literature about the life and customs of various local regions of the country.
- Postumismo (Pos-too-MEES-mo): new works of poetry and prose.

Dominican novels usually have social themes. In 1936, for example, Francisco Eugenio Moscoso wrote a novel called *Sugar Cane and Oxen* which described the sugar industry and its impact on Dominican life. Today, one of the best known writers is former president Juan Bosch, who has written more than a dozen novels and many short stories. Most of his works focus on politics or history.

"NOT ONE STEP BACK"

Pedro Mir

Pedro Mir was born in the Dominican Republic in 1913. He is a popular poet and a journalist who writes about social and political issues. He published his first books while he lived in exile between 1940 and the late 1960's. Below is part of a poem called "Not one step back"(1965). Mir ends each verse with the phrase, "Not one step back." What do you think this poet is trying to tell us by repeating this phrase so many times?

Many of Mir's poems talk about social and political conditions in Dominican history. To which events or situations could this poem be referring?

NOT ONE STEP BACK

Moon tree that responds to the climate
in a system of nocturnity,
do not let the mistletoe oppress you.
Not one step back.

Do not let the long regiment
of the years of relentless crime
touch your shoulder with the thought.
Not one step back.

May the lofty flower that sprouts from your branches
in this splash of freedom
not lose in honey even the slightest drop.
Not one step back.

Not one step back, soldiers and civilians
brothered suddenly in truth.
Life is made one above the guns,
for there are no trenches for snakes,
from our own wretches to vile foreigners.
Not one step back.

Freedom, like an ancient mirror
shattered in the light, is multiplied
and each time a fragment flashes back
the new time repeats to the old time:
Not one step back.

Not one step back, not one step back, not one step
of return to yesterday, not half
a step toward the setting sun,
not one step back.

Let nationhood—blood and sweat—
be proven in the people's fight.
Confronting the bullets with clear conscience.

And in each heart not one step back.

1965

Trans. Donald D. Walsh

DOMINICAN REPUBLIC

The map below shows the location of several agricultural products and other resources in the Dominican Republic. The lines between cities (•⌒•⌒•) show the major roads and highways.

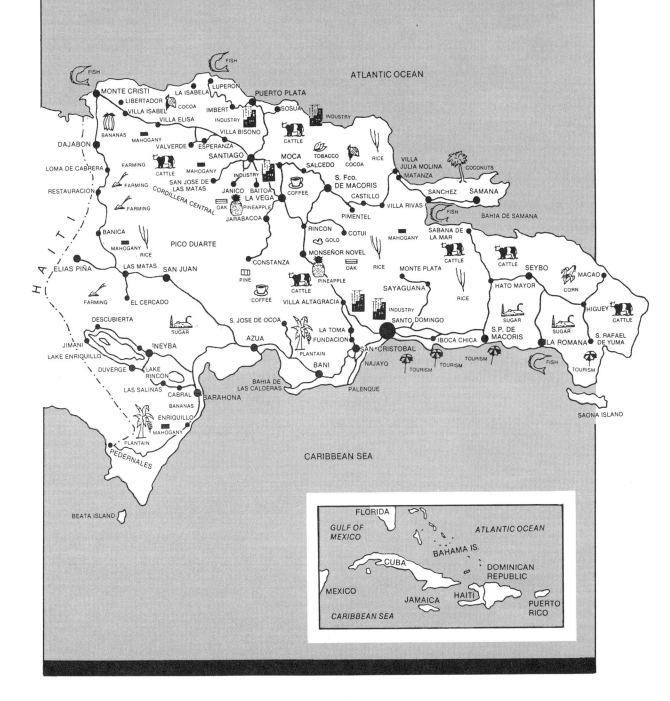

Government

Dominicans have a democratic form of government and a Constitution. Government representatives are elected every four years. There are three branches of government: the executive, the legislative, and the judicial. This form of government is similar to the government of the United States, but in the Dominican Republic the executive branch holds more power than the other two branches. Some critics of President Balaguer say that he has allowed the executive branch to gain too much power during his presidency.

Economic Life

More than 50% of the working population have jobs in agriculture. The main crop is sugar cane. Other crops are plantains, coffee, cocoa beans, corn, mangoes, avocados, tomatoes, oranges, pineapples, rice, bananas, tobacco, coconuts, and cassava.[2] In

Sugar cane is still largely harvested by hand in the Dominican Republic.

Ripe coconuts are picked by hand by someone who climbs the coconut tree.

addition, Dominicans breed cattle, goats, pigs, horses, and chickens. Mining of bauxite, gold, and silver is also important. An industry which is growing is tourism.

The Dominican Republic has economic relations with many countries. However, the United States provides the main market for Dominican sugar and other agricultural products. The government also depends on the United States for financial and technical aid, and for military training. Because the United States is the largest importer of Dominican sugar, a drop in the United States purchase of sugar has a harsh effect on the Dominican economy. When the United States buys less sugar, the

---

[2] Cassava are tropical plants with edible starchy roots. The word cassava also refers to the starch made from grated cassava (yucca in Spanish).

The sugar industry is a blend of old and new methods. Some sugar cane is carried by oxen to the mill (above left). In modern plants (above right), cane is processed into molasses, sugar, rum, and other products.

price of sugar goes down. This means that less money comes into the country, and the first result is widespread unemployment. This can quickly lead to strikes, demonstrations, political turmoil, and even violence. The same type of chain reaction can occur when the price of oil goes up in the world market. Since the Dominican Republic imports most of its fuel, a rise in the price of fuel can shut down public transportation, and cause unemployment in many other businesses. When the Dominican economy becomes unstable, large numbers of people often leave for the United States and Puerto Rico.

Although the Dominican Republic imports most of its fuel, the country produces some of its own fuel. On the left (above) is an oil and gas refinery in the Haina bay area in San Cristóbal. On the right (above) is a view of an electrical power dam in Valdesia.

The Dominican government is trying to lessen the impact of unstable sugar and oil prices on the economy. For example, the government has encouraged the growing of other products such as coffee, cocoa, tobacco, pineapples, and bananas. Officials have tried to create new jobs in areas such as construction. Dominicans hope that these efforts will help to bring about a more stable economy.

International Relations

During this century, the Dominican Republic has traded for the most part with the United States, and with other Spanish-speaking countries in the Caribbean such as Puerto Rico. Since the United States is the largest importer of Dominican products, it has a strong influence on the social, political, and economic life of the country. Some Dominicans say that this influence has caused their country to become a satellite —almost a colony— of the United States. They resent United States influence, and want to gain greater economic and political independence. Other Dominicans are in favor of United States influence. They think that aid and technology from the United States will help their country.

Since the 1960's, the Dominican Republic has expanded its trade and diplomatic relations to more than 50 nations, including Latin American neighbors such as Brazil, México, and Venezuela. Other nations such as Canada, Japan, Taiwan, West Germany, the Netherlands, Switzerland, Italy, and Spain have also increased trade with the Dominican Republic and have invested money in Dominican industry, construction, and mining. The Dominican Republic has become more important in world affairs because of these resources, and because of its central location in the Caribbean Sea. (See map on p. 4.)

Independent Picture Service

Ocean shipping is the main means of export and import in the Dominican Republic.

EDUCATION

The European style of education began in the Americas in the Dominican Republic. There, in 1538, the University of Santo Domingo was built. In the Dominican Republic today, children between the ages of 7 and 14 are required to attend school. Primary school lasts for six years. Secondary (high) school begins at age 13 and lasts for six years. More than 60% of the school-age population attends school.

The first building of the University of Santo Domingo was built in 1538 by Pope Paul II. During the colonial period, students from all parts of the Antilles attended this first university of the Americas. The building shown above still stands on its modern campus.

Eugenio María de Hostos came from Puerto Rico to live in Santo Domingo for nine years (1879-1888). He founded several schools and teachers' colleges. Eugenio María de Hostos is known for greatly improving the standard of education in the Dominican Republic.

University classroom in the city of Santiago.

FIRST VERSE OF
THE DOMINICAN NATIONAL ANTHEM
(HIMNO NACIONAL DOMINICANO)

The Dominican National Anthem was composed by José Reyes in the mid-1800's. The words were written by Emilio Prud'homme, and the music has the sound of a march. The anthem is played by military and school bands at patriotic events. Dominicans sing the anthem at events which celebrate national themes. The words of the anthem refer to Quisqueya, the original name of the Dominican Republic. Following are words and music to the first of the anthem's six verses:

Quisqueyanos valientes alcemos
Nuestro canto con viva emoción
y del mundo la faz ostentemos
Nuestro invicto glorioso pendón.
Salve el pueblo que entrépido y
fuerte, a la guerra morir se
lanzó, cuando el bélico reto de
muerte, sus cadenas de esclavo
rompió.

Valiant Quisqueyans,
Let us lift our song
with heartfelt emotion.
Let's display to the world
our invincible and glorious flag.
Let's honor the strong and courageous
people who died in combat.
They met the challenge
of war and destruction to
break the chains of slavery.[1]

República Dominicana

EMILIO PRUD'HOMME

JOSÉ REYES (1844-1863)

---

[1] Translation by R. Roland.

ción, Y del mun-do a la faz os-ten-te - mos Nues-tro in-vic-to, glo-rio - so pen-

dón. Sal-ve,el pue-blo que in-tré pi-do y fuer - te, A la gue-rra a mo-rir se lan-

zó, Cuan-do en bé - li-co re-to de muer - te Sus ca-de-nas de es-cla-vo rom-

pió.   2. Nin-gún

Dominicans in the United States

In the last twenty five years, large numbers of Dominican citizens have come to live in the United States. These Dominicans have joined the millions of people who have immigrated to this land for several hundred years.

During the Summer, the Dominican Parade is held in New York City. Even though it rained during last Summer's parade (1989), thousands of Dominicans, and other New Yorkers, came to see the floats and enjoy the music and food.

Immigration

Most immigrants have come to this country seeking better opportunities. Some have come because their religious, political, or ethnic group was under attack in their own country. Others have come looking for employment and educational opportunities. For the past several hundred years, these immigrants have helped to farm the land and to build towns, cities, roads, railroads, and industries. They have contributed their skills to the development of every profession.

Very few Dominicans immigrated to the United States and other countries until after 1960. Before then, more people came to the Dominican Republic than left for other countries. People from European, African, Asian, and other Latin American countries came to seek better economic opportunities. This was encouraged by the Dominican Republic because the country needed more workers.

Recent Immigration of Dominicans to the United States

Two events brought about the recent immigration of large numbers of Dominicans to the United States. One was the assassination of Rafael Trujillo (see p. 62). Trujillo had not allowed Dominicans to leave the Dominican Republic. After his death, there was an increase in emigration to the United States. (See chart on next page.) The other event that increased the number of Dominicans living in the United States was a change in U.S. immigration laws. These laws control the number of people who can

Photo by Luis Inocencio Vallejo

come to the United States from other countries.

In 1965, President Lyndon Johnson signed a law that removed many unfair immigration practices that discriminated against people from Latin America, Asia, Africa, and Southern and Eastern Europe. This new law also made it easier for immigrants to bring family members to the United States. For example, a son or daughter could now bring his

Table 9.1:
Dominican Migration to the United States, 1961-1981

Year	Number of Immigrants	Year	Number of Immigrants
1953-1960	922 (yearly average)	1971	12,624
1961	3,045	1972	10,670
1962	4,603	1973	13,858
1963	10,683	1974	15,680
1964	7,537	1975	14,066
1965	9,504	1976	15,088*
1966	16,503	1977	11,655
1967	11,514	1978	19,458
1968	9,250	1979	17,519
1969	10,670	1980	12,624
1970	10,807	1981	18,220

* 1976 includes an additional three months for a total of 15 months, because the INS changed its enumeration period that year.
Source: Immigration and Naturalization Service, *Annual Report*, 1954-1981.

or her mother and father, and parents could bring their children. This could be done by petitioning the Immigration and Naturalization Service to allow a family member to become a permanent U.S. resident. Thus, the Immigration Law of 1965 encouraged more Dominicans to come to the United States.

Employment in the United States

Today, you will find Dominicans living in most parts of the United States, especially in larger cities. Seventy percent of Dominicans in this country live in New York City. In fact, between 1975 and 1987, Dominicans were the largest immigrant group to come to New York City. Employment opportunities attract people to this large urban center. The protection and support of relatives who already live in New York City also encourages Dominicans to live in New York.

Dominicans work in skilled and unskilled professions. For example, many women make clothes in the garment industry. Others work in restaurants, grocery stores, and various types of factories.

Many Dominican women work in the garment industry.

87

Dominicans have also become part of the United States middle class. Some own stores, travel agencies, and factories. A bank in New York City, The Dominican Bank, is owned by Americans who are Dominican. There are Dominican doctors, nurses, police officers, lawyers, cab drivers, social workers, writers, and teachers.

Baseball Bring Dominicans to the United States

Baseball is a favorite national sport in the Dominican Republic. There are six professional teams and, during the winter months, many United States ballplayers come to the Dominican Republic to play on these teams. There are many great Dominican baseball players who play for major league teams in the United States.

These Dominican baseball players are role models for children in the Dominican Republic. Many children look up to these ballplayers who are famous and who make high incomes. Dominican children and adults spend a great deal of time playing baseball for fun. Many children hope to become baseball stars. However, only a few players are able to enter the major leagues.

Dominicans did not come to the United States to play baseball until after 1947. Up to that time, discrimination and racism prevented Black athletes from playing on major league teams. Because many Dominican baseball players were Black, they were not welcome on these teams, even if they were great ballplayers. When these unjust rules were changed,

Julio Franco is one of the best hitters among Dominican shortstops.

Many children in the Dominican Republic make their own equipment in order to play baseball.

Above are a few well-known Dominican baseball players. (Left to right) Alfredo Griffin, Julio Franco, Rafael Santana, Tony Fernández, Mariano Duncan, and José Uribe.

Dominicans began to join major league teams. Some of the first Dominicans on these teams were the three Alou brothers, Felipe, Mateo, and Jesús. Among the well known players today are Pedro Guerrero, Tony Peña, Julio Franco, Mario Soto, Rafael Santana, Jorge Bell, Juan Samuel, Tony Fernández, Mariano Duncan, José Uribe, and Alfredo Griffin. Juan Marichal, one of the best pitchers in the history of baseball, is a member of the National Baseball Hall of Fame.

The Future...

As more Dominicans continue to come to the United States, the impact of their culture will become stronger. Music, economy, and literature are just three of the areas in which Dominican influence can already be felt. The merengue, the most popular form of Dominican music, is enjoyed world-wide. In the United States, Dominicans have inspired other musicians to learn and play the merengue. In large U.S. cities, Dominicans have helped to strengthen the work force. They contribute their knowledge, services, and skills to the communities in which they live. Dominican literature, with its strong political themes, has inspired writers throughout the Americas to be part of the search for full human rights and freedom for all people.

CHAPTER 7 REVIEW

I. **Vocabulary for Review**

   A. First, put the following words in alphabetical order. Then, using the glossary at the end of the book and a dictionary, write definitions for the following words:

   environment, customs, influential, illiteracy, heritage, traditions, fertile, tourism, satellite, resent, racism

   B. Use each word in a sentence of your own. Be sure to provide good context clues for the vocabulary word.

II. **Lesson Review**

   1. List the three cultures that laid the foundation of Dominican society.
   2. Name and describe the three major groups or classes in Dominican society today. Describe three traditions that most Dominicans share.
   3. What kind of problem do Dominicans face when the price of sugar goes down and the price of oil goes up?
   4. What form of government exists in the Dominican Republic today?
   5. Why does the Dominican National Anthem refer to Quisqueya rather than to the Dominican Republic?
   6. Why did immigration of Dominicans to the United States increase after 1965?

III. **Critical Thinking and Writing**

   Culture includes elements of heritage such as language, art, religion, economy, technology, politics, and social structure. Fold a piece of paper so that it has three columns. Head column one CULTURE, and under that heading write the various elements that culture includes (language, art, religion, etc.). Head the next column UNITED STATES and the third column DOMINICAN REPUBLIC. Make a chart comparing aspects of cultures in both countries. Then, write a paragraph telling what culture includes, and how the culture of the United States is similar to or different from that of the Dominican Republic.

IV. **Enrichment Exercise**

   Make a scrapbook of Dominican baseball players. Write captions to go under all of the pictures you include.

GLOSSARY

vb = verb   *n* = noun   *adj* = adjective

abolish *vb:*   to do away with, put an end to

abolitionist *n:*   a person who spoke and argued to abolish slavery, particularly of African American people of the 19th century

annex *vb:*   to attach as an addition; to incorporate (as a territory) within a political domain

artifact *n:*   an object produced or shaped by human effort and skill; a simple tool or weapon of historic interest

assassinate *vb:*   to murder by surprise or secret attack

authority *n:*   the right to give commands and the power to enforce obedience; a fact or statement used to support a position; a person appealed to as an expert; persons having powers of government

bankrupt *adj:*   unable to pay debts

barter *vb:*   to trade by exchanging one thing for another without the use of money

blockade *n:*   the closing off of a city, coast, harbor or other area to traffic and communication by hostile ships or forces

brutal *adj:*   being cruel and inhuman

cathedral *n:*   the most important or largest church in a district headed by a bishop

colonization *n:*   the act of bringing under conquest by seeking to rule over other peoples and lands

communal *adj:*   shared among members of a group or community

communism *n:*   a set of principles aimed at establishing a society in which there is common ownership and control of the means of production

conch *n:*   an edible shellfish having no backbone and found in tropical waters

condemn *vb:*   to declare to be wrong; to pronounce guilty; to declare to be unfit for use

conflict *n:*   a prolonged struggle; battle; a clashing or sharp disagreement

convert *vb:*   to change from one belief, religion, view, or party to another; to change from one form to another; to exchange for an equivalent

custom *n:*   the usual way of doing things; a common tradition or practice

decree *vb:*   to establish by law

dictatorial *adj:*	like a dictator; overbearing; domineering; autocratic
discriminate *vb:*	to act toward a person or group on the basis of prejudice in an unjust way
doctrine *n:*	a principle, or formal statement of principles, presented for acceptance or belief.
dominant *adj:*	controlling all others; being over all others
elite *n:*	a social class with special privileges
environment *n:*	surroundings; the conditions that influence one's growth
exile *n:*	enforced removal from one's native country by an authoritative decree; banishment
expedition *n:*	a journey for a particular purpose
fertile *adj:*	rich in material needed for plant growth; capable of growing and developing; capable of reproducing
heritage *n:*	something that is passed on from one's ancestors; something that is passed on through the generations
illiteracy *n:*	the state of being unable to read or write
imaginary *adj:*	of or relating to a mental image or idea
impact *n:*	two bodies striking together; a forceful effect
influence *n:*	the power of producing an effect without apparent force of direct authority
influential *adj:*	having or exerting influence
inhabitant *n:*	one who lives in a place
interfere *vb:*	to block or stand in the way of; to hamper or stop; to intrude in the affairs of others
invasion *n:*	to enter in order to overcome by force and to conquer
isolation *n:*	the act or condition of being set apart; the condition of being kept away from outside influence
mansion *n:*	a large stately house
migrate *vb:*	to move from one country or region to another
monarch *n:*	a king or queen
navigate *vb:*	to travel by water; to steer or direct the course of a boat or plane
negotiate *vb:*	to deal with another or others in order to come to terms or reach an agreement
opponent *vb:*	one who is against another or others in a conflict, battle, contest, or debate

persecute *vb:*	to oppress or harass with ill-treatment
persuade *vb:*	to cause or convince someone to do something
population *n:*	the whole number of people in any given area; the people living in a country or region
racism *n:*	a system of oppression that controls the life chances of persons based on race
rebel *vb:*	to oppose or resist authority
recognition *n:*	acceptance of the national status of a new government by another nation; an awareness that something known has been known before; a giving of attention
regime *n:*	a form or system of government
resent *vb:*	to feel anger about something believed to be unfair, unjust, or mean
resign *vb:*	to quit; to give up
satellite *n:*	a smaller body that revolves around a planet such as earth's moon; a smaller country dominated by a larger and more powerful one
sovereign *n:*	a person such as a king or queen; one who possesses all power; self-governing and independent
staple *n:*	a chief commodity or product of a place; an important food or ingredient
survival *n:*	the condition of remaining alive; continuing to exist
symbol *n:*	something that stands for and represents something else
tension *n:*	the act of straining or stretching; a state of mental unrest
terrorize *vb:*	to fill with fear
testimony *n:*	evidence based on observation or knowledge
tourism *n:*	the practice of traveling for pleasure; the business of providing tours and services for tourists
traditions *n:*	information, beliefs, or customs that are handed down from one generation to another
tremendous *adj:*	very large in amount, extent, or degree
turmoil *n:*	an extremely confused condition
tyrant *n:*	a ruler who has no legal limits on his or her power; one who uses authority or power harshly
voyage *n:*	a trip or journey, especially by water

BIBLIOGRAPHY

Aguilar, Luis E. *Latin America: The World Today.* Washington, D.C.: Stryker-Post Publications, 1986.

Alexander, Robert J. *Latin America Political Parties.* New York: Praeger Publishers, 1973.

Alvarez, J. "An American Childhood in the Dominican Republic." *American Scholar,* vol. 56 (Winter 1987), p. 71.

Bosch, Juan. *Composición Social Dominicana.* Santo Domingo: Editorial Alfa y Omega, 1983.

Castro, J. "Harvesting Baseball Talent." *Time,* September 2, 1985, p. 42.

Charles, G.P., et. al. *Problemas Domínico-Haitianos y del Caribe.* México City: Universidad Nacional Autónoma de México, 1973.

Colón, Cristóbal. *Los Cuatro Viajes Del Almirante y su Testamento.* Madrid: Espasa-Calpe, 1982.

De Galíndez, Jesús. *Trujillo: Dominican Dictator.* Tucson: University of Arizona Press, 1973.

De Las Casas, Bartolomé. *History of the Indies,* translated by Andre Collard. New York: Harper & Row, 1971.

Domínguez, I., Castrillo, J., and Tejeda D. *Almanaque Folklórico Dominicano.* Santo Domingo: Museo del Hombre Dominicano, Editorial Alfa y Omega, 1978.

"Dominican Republic: An Investment in Stability." *Nation's Business,* vol. 71 (December 1983), p. 25.

Ecumenical Program for Interamerican Communication and Action. *The Caribbean: Survival, Struggle, and Sovereignty.* Boston: South End Press, 1985.

García, José Gabriel. *Historia Moderna de la República Dominicana.* Santo Domingo: Publications AHORA!, Tomos 1, 2, 3 y 4, 1968.

Hazard, Samuel. *Santo Domingo: Past and Present.* New York: Harper & Brothers, 1973.

Hendricks, Glenn. *The Dominican Diáspora.* New York: Center for Education in Latin America, 1974.

Knight, Melvin M. *The Americans in Santo Domingo.* New York: Vanguard Press, 1928.

Kryzanek, Michael J., & Wiarda, Howard J. *The Dominican Republic: A Caribbean Crucible*. Boulder: Westview Press, Inc., 1982.

Larrazabal Blanco, Carlos. *Los Negros y la Esclavitud en Santo Domingo*. Santo Domingo: Colección Pensamiento Dominicano, 1975.

Logan, W. Rayford. *Haiti and the Dominican Republic*. New York: Oxford University Press, 1968.

López, L. "A Hungry Mob." *Time*, May 7, 1984, p. 78.

Martin, John Bartlow. *U.S. Policy in the Caribbean*. Boulder: Western Press, Inc., 1978.

Medrano, H. "Merengue's New Moves." *Americas*, vol. 38 (September-October 1986), p. 54.

Moya Pons, Frank. *Historia Colonial de Santo Domingo*. Santiago, R.D.: Universidad Católica Madre y Maestra, 8va. Edición, 1984.

Olsen, Fred. *On the Trail of the Arawak*. Norman, Oklahoma: University of Oklahoma Press, 1974.

Pichardo, B. *Resumen de Historia Patria de la República Dominicana*. Buenos Aires: Talleres Gráficos Americalle, 1947.

Rodman, Seldon. *Quisqueya: A History of the Dominican Republic*. Seattle: University of Washington Press, 1964.

Rotberg, Robert L. *Haiti: A Politics of Squalor*. Boston: Houghton, Miffin & Company, 1971.

Rouse, Irving. "The West Indies: The Ciboney, The Carib, The Arawak." *Bulletin 143*, Washington, D.C.: Smithsonian Institute, Bureau of American Ethnology, 1948.

Thacher, John Boyd. *Christopher Columbus, His Life, His Work, His Remains*, 3 vols., New York/London: G.P. Putnam's Sons, 1903-04.

Van Sertima, Ivan, ed. *African Presence in Early America*. New Brunswick, New Jersey: Journal of African Civilizations Ltd., Inc., 1987.

Velóz Maggiolo, Marcio, et. al. *Los Modos de Vida Mellacoides*. Santo Domingo: Museo del Hombre Dominicano, 1973.

INDEX

CREDITS

We would like to acknowledge the following picture services, publishers, individuals, and other sources of materials from which illustrations and quoted materials were obtained:

Alfred A. Knopf, Inc.
Bibliográfica Omeba
Biblioteca Nacional, Madrid
Brown Brothers Stock Photos
Christoph Amberger
Citadel Press, division of Lyle Stuart, Inc.
David McKay Company, Inc., subdivision of Random House
Department of the Navy, History and Museums Division, U.S. Marine Corps
Ecumenical Program for Interamerican Communication and Action (EPICA)
Editorial El Diario
El Nuevo Diario
Enciclopédica Dominicana, S.A.
Encyclopedia Britanica, Inc.
Frank Moya Pons
Franklin Watts
G.P. Putnam's Sons
Gonzalo Briones
Holt, Rinehart and Winston, Inc.
Honorable President Joaquín Balaguer
Independent Picture Service, Lerner Publications Company
Inter-American Development Bank
Jaimes Libros
Listín Diario
Luis Inocencio Vallejo
Manuel Pareja
McGraw Hill Publications
Payson and Clarke, Ltd.
Maximo Pou
Ramco AV Productions, Richard A. Meek
Random House, Inc.
Regents Publishing Company, Inc.
Seldon Rodman
Secretaría de Estado de Turismo
Sociedad Dominicana de Bibliófilos
Sports Illustrated, Time, Inc.
Staatliche Museen
SUSAETA
Teacher's College Press, Columbia University Teacher's College
The Bettmann Archive
The Knickerbocker Press, G.P. Putnam's Sons
Tiers/Monkmeyer Press
Time-Life Books, Inc.
Tomás Pastoriza
Tony Frank
Universidad Católica Madre y Maestra
University of Washington Press
Westview Press
Vela Zanetti